Howard Fleming

NARROW GAUGE
RAILWAYS
IN
AMERICA

The bonanza boom towns of Colorado were delighted beyond compare when the proud but diminutive "Montezuma" appeared on the scene (in 1871). A new and exciting period of the glamor of railroading in America was in the making. This is a smoke-box view of the first narrow gauge passenger engine built in America by Baldwin

ORIGINALLY PUBLISHED • NEW YORK • 1875

NARROW GAUGE RAILWAYS

IN AMERICA

Howard Fleming

EDITED BY

Grahame Hardy AND *Paul Darrell*

FOREWORD BY

Lucius Beebe

INCLUDING A LIST OF NARROW GAUGE RAILWAYS
IN AMERICA • 1871 TO 1949 • COMPILED BY

BRIAN THOMPSON

NEW updated list through 1980 of Narrow
Gauge Railways in Canada, Alaska, Montana,
Hawaii, and Washington compiled by James Eakin.

PROFUSELY ILLUSTRATED WITH ENGRAVINGS
FROM ORIGINALS OF NARROW GAUGE LOCOMOTIVES,
PASSENGER AND FREIGHT CARS

†††

DECORATIONS BY **E. S. HAMMACK**

†††

Published by RAILHEAD PUBLICATIONS, Canton, Ohio
1983 • 3rd Printing

FOREWORD

There are, as this is being written, but three remaining passenger carrying narrow gage railroads in the United States, and the life expectancy of one of these is at best brief. The Rio Grande Southern, lonely and neglected monument to the nineteenth century genius of Otto Mears, "Pathfinder of the San Juan," in the desolate reaches of southwestern Colorado, may at any moment become one of the fragrant memories of yesterday's railroading in the days when the American West was filled with hope and promise. The narrow gage divisions of the rich and powerful Denver and Rio Grande Western are in much better case. The carloadings they furnish for broad gage hauls at Alamosa and Montrose achieve ponderable proportions in the railroad's economy and the cost of broadgaging them, often considered, would be prohibitive. In Pennsylvania, the East Broad Top is the property of a wealthy coal mining company and its operational limitations have been successfully integrated to the scheme of things generally so that its chances of survival are refreshingly bright.

But even in an age widowed of sentiment and quite divorced from charm in the business of railroading, the narrow gages of yesterday lay such hold upon the informed imagination and are possessed of such a rewarding wealth of legend as to justify, in the publisher's mind, the reprinting of this once standard brief for the plausibility of the three-foot railroads which our fathers knew in such fascinating abundance all the way from Maine to Old Mexico. To a generation whose own assets of sentimentality are so lean it is both refreshing and stimulating to turn to the heroic past in appraisal, admiration and a certain implicit envy.

For the three-foot railroads of yesteryear were somehow the most personal of all railroads. Their diminutive dimensions held a peculiar and warming enchantment in the collective mind of a nation dedicated to doing everything on the biggest scale imaginable. They were regarded as pets or children were regarded, with affection and delight. To ride upon them was a sort of treat, in a way as good as a theater show or going to the circus. And they are remembered with a sort of wonderment as souvenirs of a time when all the world was young. What delight to have ridden the Nantucket narrow gage from old Nantucket town to equally venerable 'Sconset in the August mornings of one's youth! What enchantment to have known the Peach Bottom which once meandered dreamily from York, still a terminal of the legendary Maryland and

Pennsylvania Railroad, to Oxford, Pennsylvania. There was wonderment and romance, by comparison to which castles in Spain were commonplace, in the names of the Crooked Creek, the Pioche and Bullionville, the Little Sawmill Run, the Bodie and Benton and the Paw Paw, the last of which flourished briefly through the meadowlands of Michigan between Paw Paw and Lawton. And there were the little Sandy River, even more bemusing by reason of its minuscule gage of two short feet, the Emlenville, Shippenville and Clarion and, of course, "Tweetsie," the wistful East Tennessee and Western North Carolina whose freight-only operations in reduced circumstances are still the admiration of the present generation of railroad connoisseurs.

Bold and sagacious General William Jackson Palmer, whose equestrian statue stands to this day in the center of Colorado Springs, is generally credited with being the father of the narrow gages in the United States, but formal history ascribes to him only the most practical of considerations in selecting the three-foot gage for the first trackage of the Denver and Rio Grande Railroad. It was cheaper to build, says the record, and available to mountain fastnesses in the Colorado Rockies impervious to the standard rails. But students of such matters know that the old gentleman was motivated by an even more prudent morality than that which was·latent in cost estimates. The custom of the times dictated the sale of sleeping space in standard gage lower berths to *two* persons, usually of the same sex to be sure, but often practically unacquainted. No such informal arrangements would be possible in narrow gage sleepers where a single occupant was none too generously accommodated. General Palmer favored, therefore, the narrow gage and the three-foot track became a symbol of morality in an age when females who, greatly daring, traveled alone aboard the cars, wore hatpins of lethal proportions as a measure of protection and armament.

Following in the pioneer footsteps of the Rio Grande, narrow gage railroads blossomed and flowered throughout the latter decades of the nineteenth century as a sort of minor cult of the dominant American religion of the period, which was railroad building. Many of them have become integral parts of the national record. In Colorado, the Denver, South Park and Pacific achieved so valiant a luster that its saga remains untarnished to this day, bright in the annals of the Rockies although its rails have long since vanished. In Nevada the Eureka and Palisade became a major commotion of its age in a very commotional commonwealth indeed. Connecting with the perpetually tumultous Virginia and Truckee, too, at Mound House, the Carson and Colorado ran from Nevada's southern mine districts across the high pass at Mount Montgomery to achieve the downlands of California's Owens Valley. There were narrow gages in Maine and Massachusetts and upper New York State, in Georgia, Oregon, Pennsylvania and Minnesota. The three-foot rails ran in seemingly illimitable parallels through the national consciousness and at the same time coiled themselves around the American heart.

That the narrow gages should, like so many other evidences and manifestations of individualist enterprise, eventually succumb to the leveling forces of standardization was probably inevitable. It is, nevertheless, an unhappy commentary on the ever crescent national urge to conformity. It would not be better for the national economy, but it would be a more reassuring index of the American character if the country were served by scores and scores of railroads in as wide a variety of gages and operational patterns. Something valid and precious disappearing from the American way of life with the coming of syndicated newspaper copy, chain grocery stores, motor cars which are altogether indistinguishable one make from another, and the universal 4' 8½" railroad gage.

The reprinting of Howard Fleming's now seemingly naïve but essentially disingenuous advocacy of the narrow gage scheme of things is more than an item of railroadiana. It is a footnote to the record of a generation which possessed more of character and individualism than is likely to be encountered again in the chronicle of human change which is so seldom the record of human progress.

LUCIUS BEEBE

Carson City, Nevada.
1949.

INTRODUCTION

Before the narrow gauges pass entirely from our time, it is considered of interest to reproduce this book — the first American work advocating the cause of the narrow gauge railroad. By narrow gauge we mean any distance between the rails less than 4' 8½". At the time of their adoption in America in the 1870's, there was considerable controversy over their advantages. In the light of present day developments the arguments in favor of them as presented by Howard Fleming, a prominent civil engineer of that pioneer time, are of significance inasmuch as the narrow gauge flourished throughout the country for well over half a century.

In the years following the Civil War, narrow gauge lines formed an important part of the American transportation scene. Within the next twenty years they had reached their peak, and for many reasons, decline followed. Powerful arguments in their favor were economy of construction, even in difficult country, and light locomotives and rolling stock. The distinct disadvantages of transshipment of goods from narrow gauge to standard gauge cars, and vice versa, plus the active enmity of the older established standard gauge lines, soon undermined the advocacy of the narrow gauge.

As our railroad system expanded, the undesirable break-of-gauge made operations more difficult for any line that was not of standard gauge. The principle of interchangeability of equipment is the backbone of the great American network. Anything that interfered with this precept was bound to be by-passed as the railroad system expanded. Consequently we are today almost without narrow gauge railroads, and their existence is a limited one at best. During the last fifty years many of the narrow gauges were standard-gauged themselves, and thus given a new hold on life, but now most of these have been absorbed in major systems or have reached the end of their track, and are to be found only in the railroad's obituary: "Abandoned."

The directory of narrow gauge railroads, compiled by Brian Thompson, contains a record of over 750 railroads of a miscellaneous nature, and shows the wide acceptance of the narrow gauge idea, in spite of all disadvantages. It is unfortunate that most of these roads have joined the legions of the past, but it is only natural they should fall victim to railroad progress, in spite of their miniature charm, and their contribution to early railroad development.

The basic text of this book is a reproduction of Fleming's second edition of 1876, simply because this edition contains much more material than the first edition of 1875, and is thus of greater value to historians. In addition to this text, there is a miscellany of narrow gauge material. Particular emphasis has been placed upon illustrations and engravings from both editions of Fleming's work, and similar pictures obtained from many sources are included with the knowledge that they will be of value. A selection of advertisements of the day — always interesting in themselves — help to round out the text. The contents are offered with the intention of filling a gap in railroad literature, especially so with the inclusion of Brian Thompson's comprehensive list, a task which has no equivalent in any other single source.

The additional material was largely obtained from periodicals of the period, and the compilers wish to express their most sincere thanks to Miss Jeannette Hitchcock of the Hopkins Transportation Library, Leland Stanford, Jr., University, for her wholehearted co-operation in the search for obscure notes from the past.

PAUL DARRELL
GRAHAME HARDY

Oakland, California, 1949.

View of spiral on Georgetown, Breckenridge & Leadville Railway, between Georgetown and Silver Plume, Colorado

Narrow Gauge Railways

IN AMERICA.

A SKETCH OF THEIR RISE, PROGRESS AND SUCCESS:

VALUABLE STATISTICS AS TO GRADES, CURVES, WEIGHT
OF RAIL, LOCOMOTIVES, CARS, ETC.

ALSO A

DIRECTORY OF NARROW GAUGE RAILWAYS

IN NORTH AMERICA.

BY

HOWARD FLEMING.

ILLUSTRATED.

SECOND EDITION:
1876.

PREFACE TO THE SECOND EDITION.

THE favorable reception accorded to the first edition of this work, through its narrating in a popular form the history of the Narrow Gauge Railway, and presenting in a succinct manner vital figures concerning those constructed, thus becoming an assistant in promoting the construction of others, must be sufficient apology for reissuing it after the lapse of a year.

In a work of this nature, devoted to a special railway interest, which is growing rapidly, the statistics require to be constantly corrected, and extensive additions made thereto, so that an annual revision is absolutely necessary in order that it may be a manual to those engaged in the promotion and construction of economical railways.

To engineers, the new chapter on construction, containing formulas for earthworks and for laying out curves, may prove useful and acceptable.

To railroad companies, the corporate history and reports of organizations other than their own may induce comparison ; and it is hoped that their relations to each other may be drawn closer by the construction of connecting roads.

To the public, whose desire for cheap means of transportation to open up rich mineral and agricultural sections, so that their latent products may be converted into wealth, and who desire to attain that end with the smallest outlay, this brochure is offered for reflection.

Forty years ago the four feet eight and a half inch gauge, the narrow gauge of that day, was opposed by the wide gauge; the antagonism was fierce, the opposition intense ; it was, nevertheless, of no long duration, and ended in the universal building of the standard gauge road of to-day. Less then a decade ago, a narrower gauge was propounded, the width be tween the rails to be three feet six inches, or less. History repeats itself. The suggestion was vigorously opposed. The partisans of each gauge availed themselves of the press, and its columns were filled with the arguments of enthusiastic exponents, until the first narrow gauge railway was constructed, when all theories were dispelled, and actual practice gave results still, as an innovation, it had to pass through its period of trial and term of probation, and submit to the severe criticism.which all must endure. This may now be considered at an end, as all attacks have ceased, owing to results having been obtained which were at first denied.

During the last twelve months narrow gauge railways have been extended and multipled in a ratio the reverse of the standard gauge—a proof of the favor in which they are held; and we anticipate from this time, that the annual mileage constructed will form a large proportion of the yearly increase of railroads in the United States.

The compiler acknowledges his indebtedness for much valuable data received from the officers of the several narrow gauge railway companies enumerated in this work, and only regrets that it was out of his power to present fuller financial statements and reports of operations. He would again impress upon railway companies the necessity of publishing this most desirable information, as its non-appearance militates not only against themselves, but the system of which they are representatives.　　　　　　　　　　　　　　　　　　　　　H. F.

Philadelphia, 1876,
311½ Walnut St.

NARROW GAUGE RAILWAYS.

DURING the early history of railways in England, a great
controversy arose among engineers as to the best gauge to be
adopted. Two eminent engineers, the greatest of the time,
Brunel and Stephenson, took opposite sides, and divided the
profession into two hostile factions, who carried on with much
energy and some acerbity of feeling what was called "the war
of the gauges." The Brunels advocated the Broad Gauge, and
the Stephensons became the champions of the Narrow. The
former gave to the Great Western line the seven-foot gauge;
the latter to the Liverpool and Manchester, and numerous
other lines, the four feet eight and a-half inch, or narrow gauge
of the period.

This controversy lasted twenty years, and every argument
that skill and ingenuity could invent was brought into requisi-
tion. Volumes were written to prove what after all had to be
determined by experience. Like most controversies, this one
at last came to an end under the accumulated evidence of
years, leaving the narrow gauge the victor—the victory having
been made decisive by the conversion of Brunel's Great Western Broad Gauge Railway to the present "standard" of four
feet eight and a half inches throughout the entire line during
1874; and in America and Canada, where a broad gauge of
six feet and five feet six inches had been adopted in some in-

stances, such as the Ohio & Mississippi and the Grand Trunk, the track has been narrowed to four feet eight and a half inches at great expense—experience having proven that the original gauge was too wide for the traffic, and that, to use the words of a celebrated engineer, the machinery and rolling stock had been built to haul and transport a gallon when they did not have more than a quart to carry. That a six-feet gauge is too wide, is demonstrated by the report of Captain Tyler on the Erie Railway, in which he recommends it to be narrowed, even though the estimated cost of effecting it amounts to $8,500,000. Further, a practical financier has stated that, " you could not raise a dollar in the United States to-day, to build a road of wider gauge than four feet eight and a half inches."

Stephenson's gauge was the result of accident or unexplained cause, as when the parts of the first locomotive were put together, it was found to fit a gauge of four feet eight and a half inches, instead of four feet nine inches, as was intended, and which was then the distance between the wheels of ordinary vehicles in England. With few exceptions, this gauge has been adhered to ever since. No one asked the question until a few years ago—Why was the present standard gauge chosen, and why will not a narrower one answer all purposes? Man is an imitative creature; and England, the birthplace of the railway, inhabited principally by a race of conservative men, has now in consequence a railway system of 16,449 miles built on the four feet eight and a half inch gauge. Although only 367 miles, according to the English Board of Trade returns, were constructed during 1874, yet Capt. Tyler, in his report, considers that the railway system is far from complete, and that many hundred miles will have to be built to give the benefit of railway communication to outlying districts. The aggregate length of railways authorized by Parliament during the years 1870, 1871, 1872, 1873 and 1874, and not yet constructed, alone amounts to more than 2,200 miles. The question that naturally suggests itself is, Why were not these railways built? The answer is, because the lines of route are not able to support a gauge costing on the average $185,000 per mile, and because capitalists are aware of the fact that more than one-sixth of the amount invested in English railroad shares pays no dividend.

This knowledge should cause the construction of the above required mileage of the narrow gauge of to-day, which, as will be hereafter shown, is built and equipped for a much more moderate figure. In fact, a pamphlet has just been issued entitled " Light Railways," urging the construction of three feet gauge railways for the convenience of small towns and villages that will place them in connection with the trunk lines. It would be absurd to advance, still more to sustain an argument for the conversion of the *present English system* to a narrower gauge; and yet, in the light of evidence, we cannot deny that a vast economy would have been made, had two-thirds of its present mileage been constructed either of the Canadian gauge of three feet six inches, the South American metre gauge of three feet three inches, or the United States standard narrow gauge of three feet; it being fully able and more than sufficient to meet all the demands of traffic *now*, and how much more when first constructed, and when the business had not attained its present proportions!

The world-famed and initial narrow gauge railway, the Festiniog, in North Wales, was originally constructed in 1832, as a horse tramway, to carry slate from the quarries to a shipping point at Portmadoc; it was made nominally of a two feet gauge, the exact gauge being half an inch less than that. This state of affairs continued until 1863, when, on the recommendation of Mr. C. E. Spooner, the engineer of the line, locomotive power was adopted. The two locomotives built for the line by Messrs. G. England & Co., in 1863, are four-wheeled engines, the wheels being two feet in diameter and coupled. The wheel base is five feet, and the cylinders which are outside are eight inches in diameter, with twelve-inch stroke. The weight of these engines, in working order, is eight tons. Subsequently, Messrs. England built five other engines of a similar class, two of them, however, being heavier, and weighing ten tons in working order. The year 1869 was marked by the introduction of the Fairlie engine, on the Festiniog railway, and the results which have since been obtained, show that Mr.

Spooner exercised sound judgment in recommending the adoption of this system. The Fairlie engine, "Little Wonder," was built by Mr. Fairlie, at the Hatcham Works, and is mounted on two steam bogies, each bogie having four coupled wheels two feet four inches in diameter. The wheel base of each bogie is five feet, and the total wheel base of the engine nineteen feet, while the weight, in working order, is nineteen and a half tons. Each bogie has a pair of cylinders $8\frac{3}{16}$ inches in diameter, with thirteen inch stroke. In ordinary work this engine will take up a train, the total gross weight, inclusive of engine, being $127\frac{1}{2}$ tons, of which about twenty-one tons will be passengers and goods carried. On the down journey, when the slate trucks are loaded and the goods wagons empty, the total weight of engine and train is about $336\frac{1}{2}$ tons, of which 230 tons are paying load.

Imperial Princes and Royal Commissions from Russia, France, Italy, Spain, Norway and Germany, together with engineers from the United States, Brazil, "and the uttermost parts of the earth," have wended their way to the Welsh hills to behold and investigate and criticise this miniature iron road. The novelty was so enduring, at first, that scarcely a week elapsed without self-appointed inquisitors presenting themselves before the chief engineer and manager of the line, Mr. Spooner, until at last he began to wonder whether he acted in that capacity or as a showman.

It may not be inopportune here to present the following abstract from the report for 1874 of the Festiniog Railway, according to the returns of the British Board of Trade:

Length of road, single track, $23\frac{1}{2}$ inch gauge, 14 miles.
Capital cost.

Paid up common stock (4% dividend in 1873), . . .	$430,930
Preferred stock (5% dividend in 1873), . . .	175,000
Loans (bearing 5% interest), ...	60,000
Total cost ($47,566 per mile), . . .	$665,930

Besides dividends and interest charges, the company paid in 1874, $6,760 for "way leave," and $1,355 for rent of lands; and adding this to the interest and dividends we have $37,102, which is $\frac{5}{57}$ per cent. of the cost of the road.

The number of passengers and tons of freight carried and receipts therefrom were :

	NUMBER.	RECEIPTS.
Passengers,	150,714	$24,555
Tons of Freight,	145,141	96,280
Other Sources,		4,145
Total Earnings,		$124,980
Working Expenses (54.04 per cent.),		67,545
Net Receipts,		$57,435

The enthusiasm provoked by the Féstiniog Railway, and the various papers issued by Robert F. Fairlie, especially those read before the British Association in 1870 and 1871, on "The Gauge for the Railways of the Future," and "Railway Gauges," has not been without effect.

On the continent of Europe narrow gauge railways are in successful operation in Belgium, France, Italy, Switzerland, Austria, Russia, Norway and Germany.

In France a plan has been set on foot for the construction of what are to be called "Rural Railroads." The project was first broached by M. Chambrier, a well known civil engineer, who has devoted much time and attention to it. The proposition is for the construction of narrow lines of "rural railroads," or a width of one metre only, instead of the usual gauge of one metre and a half—along the wide space which every traveller in France must have observed on the side of almost every high road. Now, at present, the ordinary railroads transport heavy goods at the rate of 3 or 4 centimes, or less than a cent per ton per kilometre; but only under condition of allowing a large accumulation to take place, and consequently a great loss of time at stations, and then sending off the whole in a lump by one slow heavy goods train. Now these "rural railroads," economically constructed and without stations, or depots, or accommodations of any kind, profess to be able to replace ordinary carriages, without any delays, at two or three times less than the present cost. They will connect the small towns and villages and manufactories all over the country, and carry off their produce, agricultural or other, as it is ready for transport. For their construction there will be no need of "Acts of

Parliament," or compulsory appropriations, or surveys, or other expensive preliminaries, any more than for costly contributions of any kind along the line. All that will be required will be the "concession of the roadsides" for the purpose by the Conseil-Generale of the Department, with the authority to modify here and there the inclines, when too steep. But the speed is not intended to much exceed that of an ordinary road carriage, and the trains will stop and pick up goods awaiting them at every road they cross. Simple receiving offices may be established at village stores, or the owner of goods may bring them to the train himself and accompany them to their destination, paying his fare on the way, just as in an omnibus or tramway, without the ceremony of ticket-taking or other impediment. The expense of laying down such "rural lines" will not exceed 25,000 francs per kilometre, instead of 100,000 francs, which is the case even on the most economically constructed ordinary roads in France. The estimate also of the proceeds of such lines, based on a rate of carriage of 25 centimes per ton per kilometre, and on the average road traffic of goods and passengers, seems to be fairly remunerative in a financial point of view, as an investment, exclusive of the general advantage to agricultural interests to be expected.

In Switzerland the first narrow gauge railway was opened in 1874. The maximum gradient is 201 feet to the mile, and the sharpest curve has a radius of 198 feet. The undertaking has proved very profitable. The Swiss Society for Narrow Gauge Railways, organized in September 1872, holds concessions for over one hundred miles of metre gauge railways which are now being pushed to completion.

Finally, we have to notice the narrow gauge tramways projected by the well-known Swiss locomotive engineer, Mr. A. Brunner. These are to be worked by two-storied motive power cars, and a concession has been granted for such a line from Zurich to some suburbs.

In India there are some 500 miles of the metre gauge being worked, and a considerable amount under construction. The last act, however, of the Secretary of State for India, reflects little credit upon him as a statesman, in that he has reversed

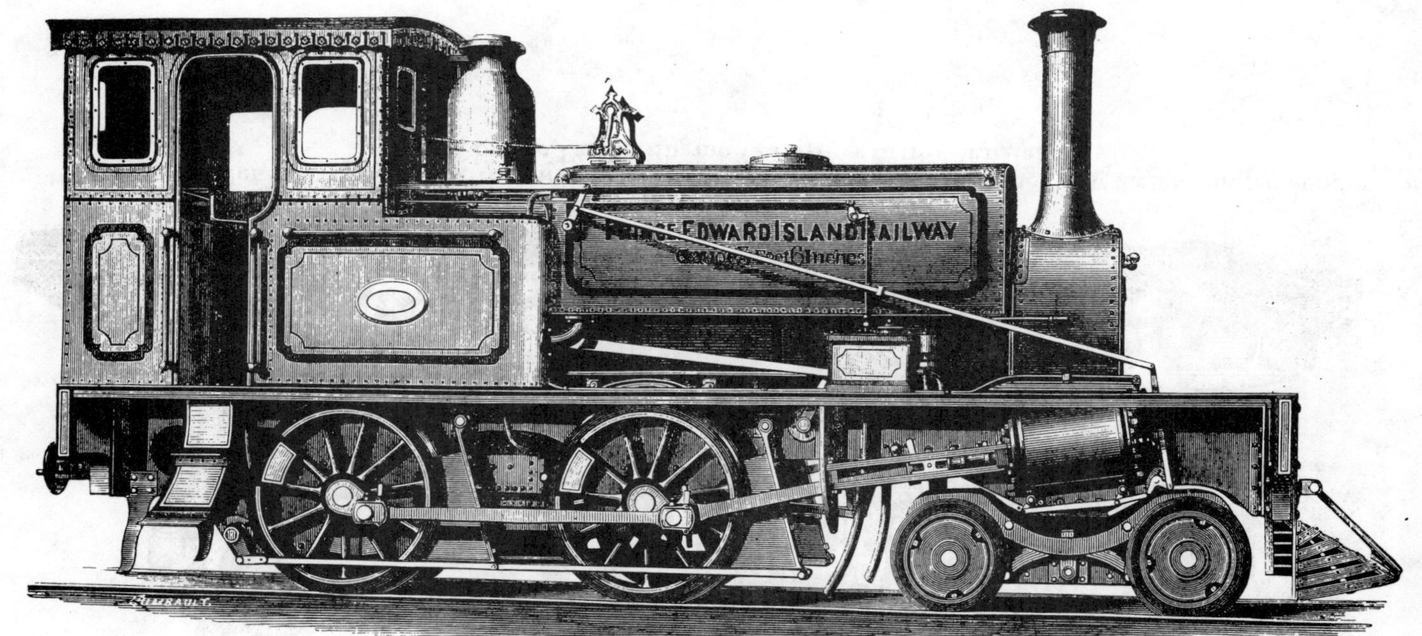

Tank locomotive for the Prince Edward Island Railway. 3′ 6″ gauge. Constructed by the Hunslet Engine Company, Engineers, Leeds, 1872

Double-boiler, double-bogie Fairlie engine for three-foot gauge. Built for the Venezuelan government railways by the Fairlie Engine Company, Bristol, England

the wise policy initiated by the late lamented Earl of Mayo, in respect to the question of the gauge of the lines to be hereafter constructed in India. We cannot but think that this decision will be reconsidered, in view of the report of the Government Director before us.

The total investment in Indian Railways is about £100,000,-000 ($500,000,000), the interest being guaranteed by the British Government on the 5,872 miles of railroad completed, which have cost on an average about $82,500 per mile.

The net earnings in 1873 were less than £3,200,000 ($16,-000,000). Without this guarantee, therefore, the investment would be very unsatisfactory—indeed, it would never have been made; and yet where the traffic grows very slowly, a gauge of five feet six inches, with its attendant heavy expenses, is persisted in to the detriment of the British Government, financially.

Were the Indian Railroad system constructed on the metre gauge, it is altogether probable that it would have been much more profitable.

In Australia and New Zealand, the narrow gauge is represented by such lines as the Queensland Railway, and the Dunedin and Port Chalmers Railway, and others.

In South America, the Argentine Confederation, the Republics on the river Plata, the Brazils and Peru, narrow gauge railways are in operation, under construction or projected. In Mexico a short line is in very successful operation.

Of the system of narrow gauge railways in Canada, New Brunswick, and British possessions in North America, we shall speak more at length, further on.

It has been reserved to the United States to carry out most fully this new departure, which originated, over forty years ago, at a secluded spot in North Wales. The object of the author is to give now the history of the rise, progress and success of the narrow gauge railway in America. No such record has yet been published. By issuing it, it is hoped to cement the relations of narrow gauge railways the one to the other, and to exhibit, in a connected form, the work done in the field and that is being still carried on. Poor's Manual of U. S. Railroads does not speak, in its preface, of the narrow gauge railways or the new system that is being introduced, and which is rapidly gaining grand proportions. Vernon's Railroad Manual likewise is silent, in its editorial and prefatory remarks, on the railroads of the United States and Dominion of Canada, in this particular; so that it behooves us, as advocates and successful demonstrators, to give to the world the results obtained since the first narrow gauge passenger railway ran its first train in America.

Before enumerating and giving a short sketch, as far as practicable, of the narrow gauge railways, a resumé of the arguments urged in their favor may not be out of place:

First. The cost of constructing a railway is nearly as the width of its gauge; in very rough countries the narrow gauge will be greatly less than the proportion to its width, whilst on flat, level ground the proportion will be more; but taking the average (excluding rolling stock, fencing, stations and telegraphs,) the cost will be found to vary as the gauge.

Second. Every inch added to the width of a gauge, beyond what is absolutely necessary for the traffic, adds to the cost of construction, increases the proportion of dead weight, increases the cost of working, and in consequence, increases the tariffs to that extent, and by that much reduces the useful effect of the railway.

Third. A saving, in first cost of construction, equal to 33 per cent., is effected, owing to the flexibility of the gauge, in allowing the road to be built so as to follow very closely the natural contour of the country, and to the reduction in graduation, bridging and superstructure. As a comparison of cost, we may take the Denver extension of the Kansas Pacific Railway, built under the same engineering supervision as the Denver and Rio Grande; the character of work on the two roads being much the same, though that of the D. & R. G. is somewhat the heaviest. The Kansas Pacific uses a rail weighing fifty-six pounds per yard; the Denver and Rio Grande using rail weighing thirty pounds per yard. Kansas Pacific cost, per mile, with equipment, $23,500. Denver and Rio Grande cost, per mile, with equipment, $13,500.

The first cost of a good Macadam highway is $6,000 a mile, and there are many narrow gauge railways that have been built and equipped for $9,000 a mile, as the annexed reports exhibit.

The following estimate of the probable cost of a narrow gauge road over a prairie country, like that around Chicago, was lately made by the railroad contractors, Messrs. F. E. Canda & Co., who built the Cairo & St. Louis Narrow Gauge Railway.

COST PER MILE—THREE FEET GAUGE.

Grading,	$2,200
Iron (30 lbs. to the yard),	4,080
Fish plates, fastenings, etc,	435
Cross ties (2,640),	800
Bridging and Culverts,	400
Track-laying and surfacing,	400
Engineering,	250
Right of Way,	300
Station Houses, Water Stations, etc.,	375
Sundries,	280
	$9,520

ROLLING STOCK.

For a road 100 miles in length, doing a coal traffic as well as general freight and passenger business, the following will be a fair equipment :

12 Freight locomotives,	$8,000	$96,000
4 Passenger locomotives,	7,000	28,000
300 Coal cars,	450	135,000
70 Flat cars,	420	29,400
100 Box cars,	520	52,000
10 Passenger cars,	3,000	30,000
3 Passenger cars, second-class,	1,500	4,500
3 Baggage cars,	1,400	4,200
Or $3,791 per mile.		$379,100

If a forty pound rail were used, the cost would be about $1200 per mile more than the above estimate; but where the grades are not steep, or the traffic especially heavy, a thirty pound rail is deemed quite sufficient.

Comparing these figures with a standard gauge road running out of Chicago, say the Chicago, Burlington & Quincy, the first cost of which we believe was about $20,000 per mile, (owing to the accounts being destroyed by the great fire of

October 9, 1871, the actual **sum cannot** be stated,) a saving is effected through the adoption of the narrow gauge of about $7,000 per mile.

About these proportions may be expected to hold good in any country not mountainous. In rough country it reaches 50 per cent., and in mountainous regions it amounts often to a diffe ence between entire practicability and impossibility, as between the two gauges.

Mr. T. E. Sickles, writing of the section of the Colorado Central Railway that passes through Clear Creek Cañon, says : "On this 13½ miles the creek falls 1,700 feet. The cost of grading a road bed through the cañon for a four feet eight and one-half inch track, was estimated to be $90,000 per mile. The *actual cost* of grading a road bed for a *three feet track*, has not exceeded $20,000 per mile. This large difference resulting from the fact that the locations of the two lines occupy different ground. On the broad gauge location the minimum radius of curvature adopted was 955 feet, and on the narrow gauge it is 220 feet. The cañon is so tortuous that the broad gauge location would have required in construction numerous tunnels and bridges across the stream, with high embankments, and deep, open rock cuttings. The adoption of the narrow gauge admitted of an alignment conforming approximately to the windings of the cañon, enabling a graded road bed to be obtained for less than one-quarter of the estimated cost of a broad gauge road bed, with the additional advantage that increase of distance secured more favorable grades."

Further, the equipment is adapted to the gauge and the requirements of traffic. Lighter locomotives and rolling stock being made use of, entails consequently a lighter rail.

Fourth. The dead weight of trains, conveying either passengers or goods, is in direct proportion to the gauge on which they run ; or in other words, the proportion of non-paying to paying weight (as far as this is independent of management) is increased exactly as the rails are farther apart ; because a ton of materials disposed upon a narrow gauge is stronger, as regards its carrying power, than the same weight when spread out over a wider basis. In proof of this we need only cite the

case of the Festiniog Railway. · The wagons used upon it, for carrying timber, weigh only 12cwt., and they frequently carry a load of over 3½ tons, at a speed of twelve miles an hour. In other words, these wagons carry as much as six times their own weight, whilst the best wagons on the ordinary English gauge do not carry as much as twice their own weight.

On the Denver and Rio Grande the freight cars weigh less than three tons, and carry a paying load of eight tons, being nearly three times their own weight, whilst on American standard roads it is generally one to one.

The following figures from the Louisville and Nashville Railroad Company, show the proportion of dead weight to paying load on their average passenger train :

	Dead weight.	Paying weight.	Tons of dead to one of paying.
Main Stem, ...	163.54	6.21	26.33
Knoxville Branch, . .	115.12	5.58	20.63
Memphis Line, . . .	153.19	4.64	33.01
Nashville & Decatur Div., .	126.43	3.19	39.62
Bardstown Branch, . . .	99.86	3.33	30.00
Richmond Branch, . .	87.28	1.62	53.88
Glasgow Branch, . . .	65.53	1.69	38.12

The disproportion of dead weight to paying load has become so noticeable, that the president of the Master Mechanics' Association referred to it in his last annual report, from which we make the following extract :

Gentlemen, the railway bankruptcy has given rise to various expedients for overcoming it. Among other remedies, "narrow-gauge railways" have been recommended as capable of so much cheaper operation that their adoption would work a cure. I refer to this, not for the purpose of discussing the question of gauge, but to call your attention to the fact that where the narrow gauge has been adopted the great practical effect has been to materially reduce the weight of the rolling stock.

Here, gentlemen, it is well we should pause for reflection ; here we are touched in our own department of railway economy ; here we are affected where we alone are concerned, and where we have the whole responsibility. If a narrow-gauge railway can be operated at materially less expense than one of the ordinary gauge, chiefly because the rolling stock in use upon it is lighter, or, to speak more correctly, there is less dead weight hauled upon the narrow gauge in proportion to the paying weight, is there not a remedy at once to be applied to reduce the cost of doing business on railways of the ordinary gauge by reducing the weight of the rolling stock ?

Gentlemen, during the last twenty years railways of the ordinary gauge have not changed in their superstructure, in their bridges, or in their iron, but the rolling stock in use upon them has increased in weight from fifty to one hundred per cent., and the usual load for a freight car has increased fifty per cent. The same bridge and the same iron, and yet an enormous increase in the weight which is constantly bearing down to crush that iron and those bridges. Gentlemen, can any thing be more obvious than that if the proper proportions formerly existed between the superstructure, the iron, and the bridges, and the weight of the rolling stock, those proportions are now entirely out of balance?

If a locomotive that weighed twenty-two tons, a freight car that carried eight tons, and a passenger car that weighed fifteen tons, were suitable to the ordinary gauge of railways twenty years ago, how is it that, without changing the roads, we are now operating on them locomotives weighing thirty-three tons and upward, freight cars loading twelve tons and upward, and passenger cars varying from twenty to thirty-five tons?

I believe, gentlemen, that these are essentially the facts of the case. I believe they have had a material influence in producing the present railway bankruptcy, and it seems to one that it does not speak well for our influence as master mechanics that we have not been able to do more with railway managers in preventing the use of rolling stock of such enormous weight.

Fifth. Traffic capacity. The evidence furnished by several commissions, establishes beyond question that the four feet eight and a half inch gauge possesses a capacity far greater than is needed.

The Massachusetts Railroad Commissioners, in their seventh annual report, state that the average number of passengers to each train during the last year was 66, and the average number of tons of freight was 64. The passenger trains, including locomotives and baggage-cars, averaged 122½ tons of dead weight, and the freight trains, 212½ tons. Taking each train as consisting of four passenger cars, we have an average of 16 to each car, when they are constructed to carry 56. Consequently, the returns would seem to indicate that the railroad corporations of the State haul 1.77 tons of rolling stock for each passenger they carry, and 3.29 tons for each ton of freight.

A narrow gauge passenger car weighing, say 15,000 pounds, is constructed to carry 36 passengers. We will presume for an instant that they only carry on the average 10 passengers, being the same proportion as 16 is to 56; an unproductive weight capacity (including engine and tender 45,000 pounds,) is, therefore, carried of 1.08 tons for each passenger, being

1,600 pounds less than the standard gauge; but this is a presumption that rarely or never occurs, the cars being most frequently more than half occupied, so that the dead weight proportion is considerably reduced.

Touching freight capacity, the following letter is produced, which speaks for itself. This effectually disposes of the theory that the narrow gauge cannot compete with the broad one:

DENVER, COLORADO, Aug. 20, 1873.

W. W. Borst, Esq., Superintendent Denver & Rio Grande Railway:

DEAR SIR:—It was with some doubts that I applied to you for transportation for my Great World's Exposition, consisting of circus, menagerie and aquarium, over your line, it having been intimated to me that great difficulty might be experienced in obtaining sufficient accommodations over the *Narrow Gauge*, and even if these were obtained, it would be extremely hazardous, as many of my cages of animals are very high. I have had several years experience in transporting my circus, etc., over railroads, and I desire hereby to express to you my appreciation of your arrangements made for us, and to say that never has my World's Exposition been moved more promptly or satisfactorily, your cars being ample to accommodate my stock, wagons, cages and even the elephant, weighing five tons and standing nine feet eight inches in height. The stock and animals have never ridden on any line with as much ease and comfort as on your *Narrow Gauge* road. Your cars being so near the ground, renders them much easier to load than those of the ordinary gauge. I have met with courteous and business-like treatment from your employees and agents, and everything was a complete success.　　　　　　　　　　Truly Yours,

[Signed]　　　　　　　　　　　　　　JOHN ROBINSON, JR.,

Manager Old John Robinson's Great World's Exposition.

Sixth. Economy in management. In this respect the narrow gauge railway shows a marked advantage, the cost of operating being about twenty per cent. under that of a standard gauge road. The Utah Northern Railway reports expenses as 56.2 per cent. of the gross earnings; the Toledo and Maumee, as 50 per cent.; the Toronto and Nississing, 61.25 per cent.; the Mineral Range, 63.56 per cent. For the comparison of a narrow gauge railway with one of standard width, we can take the Cairo and St. Louis and the St. Louis and Southeastern, which run parallel for some distance. Owing to the competition of the narrow gauge, the St. Louis and Southeastern was obliged, during 1875, to pass its interest. Comment is unnecessary.

In comparing the wear and tear of the two gauges, the advantage is immensely in favor of the narrow gauge, with its light machinery and rolling stock. The ordinary standard gauge passenger car, weighing 35,000 pounds empty, hammers the rail joints with 4,375 pounds on each wheel, when loaded and hauled over the rail at twenty-five or thirty miles per hour; the weight of the blow is enormous, and terribly destructive to the superstructure.

A first-class narrow gauge passenger car weighs 15,000 pounds, empty, and consequently only hammers the rail with 1,875 pounds per wheel.

The same truth applies to locomotives. A thirty-ton locomotive, and its loaded tender weighing about seventeen tons, or a total of forty-seven tons, will exert a pressure of nearly six tons on each driving wheel. When driven at a high speed the strain upon the track is terribly destructive.

The narrow gauge railway uses locomotives weighing from eight tons up to engines weighing forty two tons. The weight being distributed over the driving wheels, thereby gaining the necessary adhesion and requisite power, a greater paying load can be hauled, either on a level or up a grade, than on the broad gauge.

To exemplify this, Mr. Richard B. Osborne, a civil engineer, has prepared the following table, assuming the very largest class of locomotives put on the three feet gauge, with cylinders of fifteen by eighteen, thirty-six inch drivers and thirty tons weight, and with a tractive power, on a level, equal to 1,460 tons, so as to compare it directly with an engine of equal power on the standard road.

On a level—gross weight of train 1460 tons.

	Tons.
The 3 feet engine with 399 tons of cars will haul of coal, . .	1064
The 4 feet 8½ inch engine with 566 tons of cars will haul of coal, .	900

On a maximum grade of 26 4-10 feet, gross weight being 587 tons:

	Tons.
The 3 feet engine with 160 tons of cars will haul of coal, . .	427
The 4 feet 8½ inch engine with 226 tons of cars will haul of coal, .	361

On a maximum grade of 40 feet, gross weight being 444 tons:

	Tons.
The 3 feet engine with 121 tons of cars will haul of coal, . -	323
The 4 feet 8½ inch engine with 171 tons of cars will haul of coal, .	273

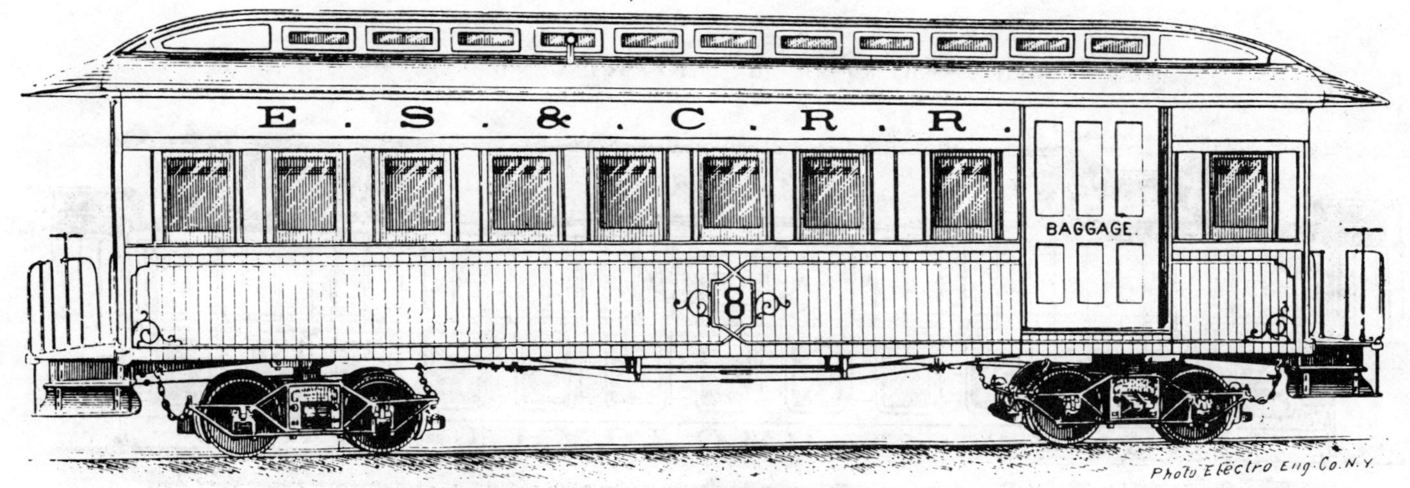

Combination passenger and baggage car of the Emlenton, Shippenville and Clarion Railway, 1877

Passenger car "Olean" of the Olean, Bradford & Warren Railway, 1878

These trains, it will be seen, *correspond in gross weight :* the three feet gauge by its *less* weight of cars transporting about seventeen per cent. *more* productive *load* than the standard gauge.

On a gradient of 80 feet per mile, gross weight 252 tons :

	Tons.
The 3 feet engine with 70 tons of cars, will haul of coal, . .	182
The 4 feet 8½ inch engine with 97 tons of cars, will haul of coal, -	155

From the foregoing we learn :

First. That an engine of 3 feet gauge can take a *greater number of tons* of freight in its cars against the same grade; and

Second. That it will haul the *same number* of tons of load in its cars up *steeper grades* than the engines of the 4 feet 8½ inch gauge, with *its* loaded cars, can at all accomplish.

We have shown before that the load of freight on the 4 feet 8½ inch against a $26\frac{4}{10}$ grade is 361 tons, and that this *freight* load can be increased on the 3 feet gauge to 427 tons against a like grade; so also can it be stated that the freight load of 361 tons, not being increased on the 3 feet road, it could be taken by the narrow gauge engine over 33 feet grades instead of $26\frac{4}{10}$ feet. A gain in gradient obtained of 25 per cent. by the adoption of the 3 feet gauge.

So likewise the freight load of the 4 feet 8½ inch engine on a gradient of 80 feet being 155 tons; that of a three feet would be 182 tons. But giving the 3 feet engine the load only of its rival, or the 155 tons, it will transport it over grades of 95 feet, or about 20 per cent. greater.

It seems then clear that while the *steam power* of the 3 feet gauge engine is *no greater* than the other, and keeping the *same paying loads* as the wider gauge, the smaller road can overcome gradients from 20 to 25 per cent. greater.

Under the caption of "Locomotives" will be found some further remarks on the power of narrow gauge engines. We therefore leave this subject for the present.

Seventh. Safety. During the early discussion of the relative merits of the standard and narrow gauge railway, the question as to safety on the narrow gauge was propounded, and it was boldly asserted at the time that it would be extremely hazardous to ride in cars the wheels of which were only three feet apart, and that if they were hauled at a velocity equal to the cars on the ordinary gauge, it would be courting certain danger. It was the old argument, in another form, against the first introduction of steam locomotion. That the hypothesis was fallacious is evidenced in the fact that *since the first narrow gauge train commenced running in America, there has been no serious accident entailing great loss of life reported.* We leave it to our readers to compare this statement with the record of standard gauge railroads.

A Porter-built 0-6-0 for the Sierra Lumber Company, which was built to the unusual gauge of 3' 3½", at Lyonsville, California

CONSTRUCTION OF NARROW GAUGE RAILWAYS.

"THE first object for consideration in examining a project for a railway is the nature and extent of the traffic to be provided for. If this is large and of a character to demand high speed, the work must be adapted to bear the contemplated service. *If a light traffic, and especially with a lower rate of speed, is anticipated, much may be saved in the expense of construction, and also in the expense of operating the railway by adapting the works to the service to be performed.*" Such are the opening words of a book on railway property published sixteen years ago, before a narrower gauge than four feet eight and a-half inches was contemplated, and the words we have italicised are peculiarly applicable to the narrow gauge system. In fact, they are the text which its exponents have always quoted.

A narrow gauge railway should not be built where a heavy traffic is expected or a high rate of speed demanded, as under those circumstances the standard gauge should be laid down, but where a country has to be developed by a railway transporting its products to a market, and where the development will take time, and the community are unable to raise the capital for and support a standard gauge, then the narrow gauge railway is the one to adopt. If these principles are not adhered to at the outset, complications will arise which could have been avoided at the first, and we may safely assert that if many of the railways now in default had been constructed of the narrow gauge, the country would not be suffering from the depression which commenced after the panic of 1873.

It is argued by those opposed to the narrow gauge, that light standard gauge railways can be constructed and equipped for the same cost as narrow gauge roads ; and that break of gauge and transhipment would thus be obviated. An examination of the argument, shows that the earthworks for a light standard gauge railway cannot be less than those of a railway of same gauge, doing a heavy through business, as the dimensions of cuts, banks, and tunnels are not reduced. There is, therefore, no saving under this head. In bridging and trestling a small saving might be effected, provided that the cars for the light standard gauge are only permitted to pass them. Cross ties would remain of same dimensions. In iron a forty-five pound rail could be adopted, which would save a trifle. In rolling stock, the greatest saving could be effected, but not to the extent that it is urged; and in comparison with the narrow gauge, would be much weaker.

On the other hand, a light standard gauge railway would run its cars over its main line connection, and endeavor to prevent them being made up in trains with heavier rolling stock—an impossibility, and the result would be the demolition of the weaker. Or goods received on main line in a heavy car are consigned to some point on the light railway, when either the superstructure must be injured or transhipment take place. There is, therefore, no real economy in their construction, whilst in the narrow gauge a saving of 33% can be effected.

The duty of location is a very important one too often overlooked. The alignment being diverted for the gratification of individuals whereby the public suffer. Due consideration must also be given to the general line of the trade of the district which the railway is to pass through, as if it crosses it at or near right angles it is seldom a success. In this respect we quote the following from the report of the Erie Railway in 1853. "Experience has now demonstrated that no more safe or profitable investment can be made in this country than in a well located and well managed railway."

In the proper location of the line the grades, curves and earthwork require very careful attention, especially when the railway is to be of narrow gauge and constructed economically. We shall consider these in their order.

GRADES AND GRADING.

The narrow gauge aims at following as closely as possible

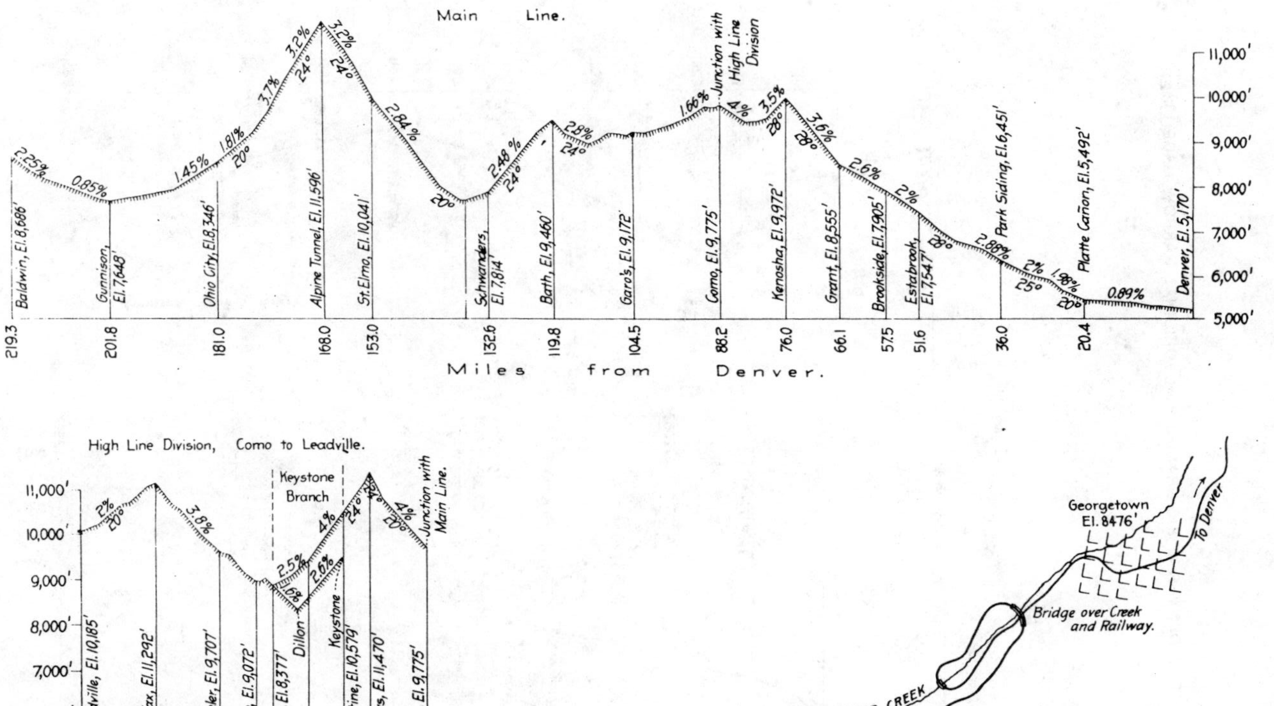

PROFILE OF THE DENVER, LEADVILLE & GUNNISON RY.

Main Line.
11,000'
10,000'
9,000'
8,000'
7,000'
6,000'
5,000'
Baldwin, El.8,686'
2.25%
Gunnison, El.7,648'
0.85%
Ohio City, El.8,346'
1.45%
1.81%
20°
3.7%
24°
3.2%
3.2%
24°
Alpine Tunnel, El.11,596'
St.Elmo, El.10,041'
2.84%
20°
Schwanders, El.7,814'
2.48%
24°
Bath, El.9,460'
2.8%
24°
Garo's, El.9,172'
1.66%
Junction with High Line Division
Como, El.9,775'
4%
3.5%
Kenosha, El.9,972'
28°
28°
3.6%
Grant, El.8,555'
2.6%
Brookside, El.7,905'
2%
Estabrook, El.7,547'
2%
2.88%
Park Siding, El.6,451'
2%
25°
1.98%
Platte Cañon, El.5,492'
20°
0.89%
Denver, El.5,170'
219.3   201.8   181.0   168.0   153.0   132.6   119.8   104.5   88.2   76.0   66.1   57.5   51.6   36.0   20.4
Miles   from   Denver.

High Line Division,   Como to Leadville.
11,000'
10,000'
9,000'
8,000'
7,000'
6,000'
5,000'
2%
20°
3.8%
Keystone Branch
2.5%
2.6%
4%
24°
24°
4%
20°
Junction with Main Line.
Leadville, El.10,185'
Climax, El.11,292'
Wheeler, El.9,707'
Frisco, El.9,072'
Dickey, El.8,377'
Dillon
Keystone
Argentine, El.10,579'
Boreas, El.11,470'
Como, El.9,775'
151.1   137.4   126.1   119.9   116.4   103.7   98.7   88.2
Miles   from   Denver.

Georgetown El.8476'
To Denver
Bridge over Creek and Railway.
CLEAR CREEK
Silver Plume
El.9176'
To Graymont
Grade 3.5%
The Georgetown Loop, U.P.D. & G. Ry.

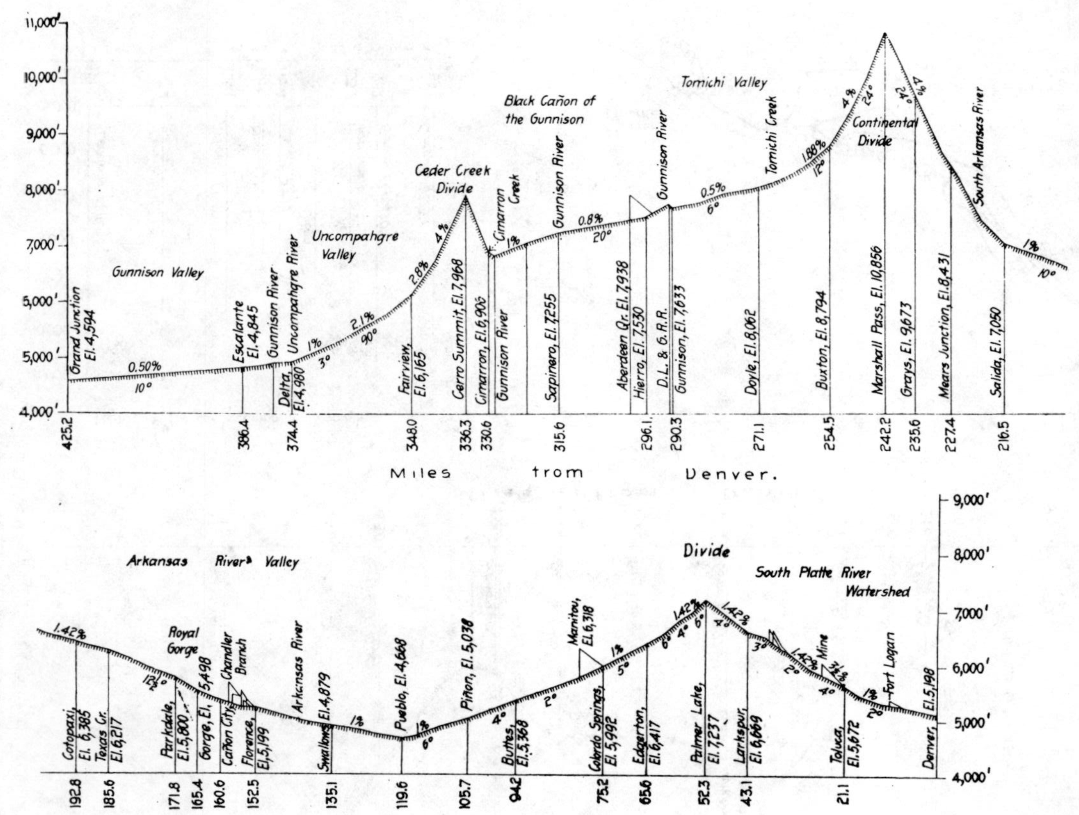
PROFILE OF THE DENVER & RIO GRANDE R. R. (ORIGINAL NARROW GAGE LINE).
Gunnison Valley
Grand Junction El. 4,594
Escalante El. 4,845
Gunnison River
Delta, El. 4,980
Uncompahgre River
Uncompahgre Valley
Fairview, El. 6,165
Ceder Creek Divide
Cerro Summit, El. 7,968
Cimarron, El. 6,905
Cimarron Creek
Gunnison River
Black Cañon of the Gunnison
Gunnison River
Sapinero, El. 7,255
Aberdeen Qr. El. 7,938
Hierro, El. 7,530
D.L. & G.R.R.
Gunnison, El. 7,633
Doyle, El. 8,062
Tomichi Creek
Tomichi Valley
Buxton, El. 8,794
Continental Divide
Marshall Pass, El. 10,856
Grays, El. 9,673
Mears Junction, El. 8,431
South Arkansas River
Salida, El. 7,050
0.50%
10°
1%
90°
3°
2.1%
2.8%
4%
1%
0.8%
20°
6°
0.5%
12°
1.88%
4%
24°
24°
4%
1%
10°
Miles   from   Denver.
425.2
386.4
374.4
348.0
336.3
330.6
315.6
296.1
290.3
271.1
254.5
242.2
235.6
227.4
216.5
Divide
Arkansas River Valley
South Platte River Watershed
1.42%
Royal Gorge
Chandler Branch
Cañon City
Florence, El. 5,199
Gorge, El. 5,498
Parkdale, El. 5,800
Arkansas River
Swallows El. 4,879
Pueblo, El. 4,668
Piñon, El. 5,038
Buttes, El. 5,368
Manitou, El. 6,318
Colorado Springs, El. 5,992
Edgarton, El. 6,417
Palmer Lake, El. 7,237
Larkspur, El. 6,669
Mine
Fort Logan
Toluca, El. 5,672
Denver, El. 5,198
Cotopaxi, El. 6,385
Texas Cr. El. 6,217
1.42%
12‰
0°
1%
1%
6°
4°
2°
5°
1%
4°
6°
4°
6°
1.42%
1.42%
4°
3°
1.42%
2°
4°
3½°
3½°
1%
2°
9,000'
8,000'
7,000'
6,000'
5,000'
4,000'
192.8
185.6
171.8
165.4
160.6
152.5
135.1
119.6
105.7
94.2
75.2
65.6
52.3
43.1
21.1

the contour of the ground over which it passes, thereby avoiding the expensive cuts, and fills, and tunnels which so much advance the cost of construction. It has been frequently stated that a narrow gauge locomotive with its train of cars can surmount much steeper grades than the standard gauge locomotives. This is only true as regards paying load, which we have exemplified on page 18. We would recommend that moderate grades be only used, and where it is necessary to have long steep grades that short levels be introduced so that a continuous grade may be avoided. By this means the engines will be relieved and the summit more easily attained.

One of the most important points that require attention in grading, is the drainage, this being essential to a good railway; as if this is not provided for, the track will settle unequally, and a disagreeable rolling motion will be experienced when riding over it, which imparts a feeling of insecurity and gives the railway a bad name. When the line passes over comparatively level country, it is always prudent to secure good drainage by raising the grade a few inches above the surface ground, even if first expense is increased. It will also avoid the constant tamping and surfacing which would otherwise occur. For width of road-beds in cuts twelve feet is found to answer and on banks ten feet is sufficient

CURVATURE.

This feature in the construction of a narrow gauge railway, to a great extent, controls the reduction in earthwork and tunneling, and demands the fullest attention. We cannot too highly impress the necessity of properly laying them out as they affect the wear of rolling stock and safety of travel owing to their being so much sharper than on the standard gauge. Henck's Field Book so fully treats on curvature, that it is unnecessary to go into detail on this head, but we present the following formula originated by G. H. Mann, C. E., which will be found useful in laying out curves of small radius, as the method of laying out by deflection is often inconvenient, owing to the chords being short and inconveniently close to the instrument.

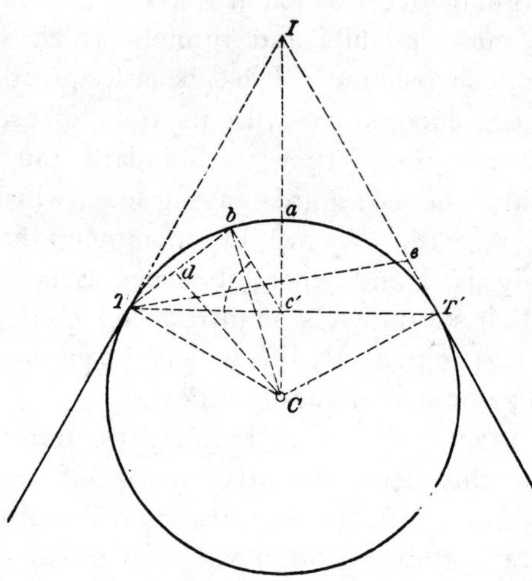

The random line T e is first run, and the angle I found by measuring I e T and I T e, and taking their sum from 180°. Then I T T′ determined, and the chord T T′ located. On this middle point, c' is taken as the station. Then if we lay off any line c' b, making an angle I with the chord, the distance on this line to the circle will be

$$d = b\,c' = \sqrt{R^2 - h^2}\cos I - h \sin I. \qquad (1)$$

$$R = \text{radius of circle} = \frac{\tfrac{1}{2}\,\text{chord}}{\sin I\,T\,T'} \text{ or } \frac{T\,c'}{2\sin I\,T\,T'};$$

$$h = c'\,C = \tfrac{1}{2}\,\text{chord} \times \tan I\,T\,T';$$
$$\text{or } T\,c' \times \tan I\,T\,T'.$$

This value (1) may be determined as follows :

$$x^2 + y^2 = R^2 \qquad . \qquad . \qquad . \qquad (2).$$
$$x = d \cos I, \; y = d \sin I + h.$$

(2) becomes

$$d^2 \cos^2 I + d^2 \sin^2 I + h^2 + 2\,d\,h \sin I = R^2.$$
$$d^2 + 2\,d\,h \sin I = R^2 - h^2.$$
$$d + h \sin I = \sqrt{R^2 - h^2 + h^2 \sin^2 I}.$$
$$d = \sqrt{R^2 - h^2}\cos^2 I - h \sin I.$$

Or we may, if stakes are to be set at equal distances along the curve, proceed as follows :

$$\text{Let } T\,b = V \; <)\, T\,c\,b = a, \; b\,T\,c' = \beta.$$

$$\text{Then } a° = \frac{l}{2\,\pi\,R} \times 360°, \text{ and}$$

$$\tfrac{1}{2}\,a° = <)\,T\,c\,d \text{ or } b\,T\,I = \frac{l}{\pi\,R} \times 90° =$$

$$\frac{l}{R} \times 28° \, 39' \,; \text{ then}$$

$$\beta = I\,T\,T' - \tfrac{1}{2}\,a.\; d^2\; \overline{T c'}^2 + \overline{T b}^2 - 2\,T\,c\,T\,b \cos \beta,$$

$$\text{or if } c = \text{chord}, \; d = \sqrt{\tfrac{1}{4}\,c^2 + l^2 - c\,b \cos \beta}\,;$$

and angle I is found thus :

$$\sin I = \frac{l \sin \beta}{d}.$$

It will be noticed that the exact length of each arc is laid out, and no error arises from the chord being taken equal to the arc. For curves of small radius, and where the length of arc is required to be quite small, this method has the advantage that the instrumental work can be done very rapidly.

Regarding the proper elevation of outer rail on curves, I find it to be the practice on some roads to leave the degree of elevation to the section men, they putting them up according to *taste*. The consequence is that some curves are nearly "flat" or level, while others are "stuck clear up," and cars will pass around some of them very smoothly at high rates of speed, while on others the oscillation is fearful. Recent observation discloses the fact that on a curve *properly* elevated there is *no oscillation*, however great the speed, providing always the track is in good surface and line. If the elevation is too great, the wheel flanges will be thrown against the inner rail with great force at high velocities. This may be accounted for in various ways.

One prominent engineer charges it to the cone of the wheels, and claims that the coning of wheels is an erroneous practice. This needs further investigation before mechanics will consent to drop the cone, the prevailing opinion being that the plan is correct. The idea is that in passing around a curve, the larger diameter of the wheel treads the rail on the outer side, while that on the inner, having a less distance to travel, runs on its smaller diameter, which seems to accord with both theory and practice. The evil ascribed to the cone as producing oscillation is doubtless chargeable to imperfections in the track. This is apparent from the fact that *there is no oscillation on a perfect track on curves*. In running at high velocities on curves, a slight imperfection in the line has a tendency to throw the flange against the inner rail, which of course puts the inner wheel on its largest diameter on the *short side of the curve, where it should not be*. The reaction of the powerful side thrust, together with the natural tendency of the cars to fall on the outer rail, brings it suddenly back to its former bearing, when there is another reaction, which is greatly assisted by an excessive elevation of the outer rail by the force of gravity. Thus we see that by the combined action of gravity, centrifugal force and momentum, aided by imperfection in the permanent way, oscillation will continue entirely around the curve when the wheel is once thrown from its proper place on the rail by a single imperfection in the track on first encountering the curve, although the rest of the curve may be in perfect condition, The same imperfection in the permanent way that will throw the flanges against the inner rail on an elevated curve will do the same thing on a "flat" curve, but with somewhat diminished force, owing to the lack of aid from gravity, as in the case of the elevated rail. But while the inward end thrust is made more forcible by the action of gravity on the elevated curve, that is to say by its (the axle) running down hill, the reaction on the flat curve is greater and throws the wheel flange against the outer rail with greater force, as the motion is on a plane instead of on an incline or up-hill. In this way the danger of derailment is far greater on the flat than on the elevated curve. A defective joint, a worn flange, or any slight imperfection, may cause the wheel to mount by the undue force with which the wheel flange is thrown against the outer rail by the centrifugal force and reaction above mentioned. As the outer rail is the *guide* for the wheels, it is important that it be kept in a condition as nearly perfect as possible, both in regard to its surface and line, as well as its elevation. It is also noticeable that on most roads the rails are not sufficiently bent on sharp curves, which causes excessive oscillation and wear, and this should receive greater attention than is usually the case. The proper way is to commence the elevation 100 feet before reaching the P. C. This gives an easy approach to the curve, as the wheel flange always follows the higher rail on straight line, and by reaching the curve with a gentle elevation, the wheels get their proper position against the outer rail, when they will keep it entirely around the curve unless forced inward by causes above mentioned.

CROSS TIES.

Ties 5 inches by 7 inches, by 7 feet long, and placed two feet apart from centre to centre, give sufficient bearing surface.

RAILS.

The weight of iron is governed by the heaviest weight on

any single wheel; this is invariably on driving wheels of engines, and by the amount of traffic. Some narrow gauge railways have found a 25 pound iron rail sufficient, while others use a 56 pound rail, or lay down a 40 pound steel rail at first. The majority use 30 and 35 pound iron rail. A few companies, unable to purchase iron at the outset, have availed themselves of wooden rails, made of hard maple, set into the ties, which are notched to receive them, and made fast by wooden keys. The rails are 3½ inches by 6 inches, and as long as they can be got, and are spliced with a lap joint, held fast by two bolts. The wear of rails thus far has not been sufficient to furnish statistics in reference to their life on grades and curves.

TRACK-LAYING.

Mr. Huntingdon has so tersely written on this subject, that we give his words entire:

Track-laying is generally performed in a careless manner, with little or no regard to wear and tear of track and rolling stock. The main object in view being to get over the ground as fast as possible, so as to put the road in operation, when all defects may be remedied. This might be well enough if the remedy was sure to be applied, but this is very seldom the case, and track once poorly laid, is generally allowed to remain so until safety demands a thorough overhauling, which can only be done at great expense and inconvenience. Indeed, there is no remedy for some of the defects of poor track laying after the road is put in operation. Of course the ballasting can be done, the track put in good surface and line, the ditches and water courses cleaned out, and the road put in good running order, for the *present;* but if the ties are improperly laid, crooked iron laid on a straight line, if the iron is not sufficiently curved on curves, or is allowed to run ahead on curves, the inner rail getting so far ahead as to bring the joint-ties diagonally across the track, there is no remedy, except to tear up the track and relay it.

PROGRESS OF NARROW GAUGE RAILWAYS.

Although narrow gauge railways in the United States are comparatively new, it being only five years since the ground was broken—in 1871—for the initial line, the Denver & Rio Grande Railway, yet a large amount of mileage can be shown as completed and under speedy construction, notwithstanding the strong opposition and prejudice against them at their first introduction. That the opposition is declining and the prejudice being overcome, is evident in the fact that such first-class standard gauge lines as the Pennsylvania, the Lehigh Valley, the Philadelphia, Wilmington and Baltimore, and the Memphis and Charleston, recognize in narrow gauge railways important adjuncts and feeders to their trunk line, and have assisted in their completion by either supplying superstructure or equipment, or guaranteeing, as in the case of the Philadelphia, Wilmington and Baltimore, and Baltimore Central to the Peachbottom Narrow Gauge Railway, a commission of 25 per cent. for the first year, and 20 per cent. for the second year, etc., on all passengers or freight carried by them, which is recarried over the Peachbottom road from their country, or consigned from Philadelphia or Baltimore to points in the country reached over the Peachbottom.

That the attention of the public has been directed to the matter—a pressing want being felt that by some practicable means cheaper modes of transportation may be obtained, more particularly in and for those sections not now furnished with a ready means of forwarding, to a market, the comparatively small amount of surplus available for export, but having such means at command could and would rapidly develop resources which otherwise must remain dormant—is evidenced by the annexed table giving the mileage constructed during each of the five years 1871–5 :

NARROW GAUGE RAILWAYS IN OPERATION.

STATE OR TERRITORY.	NAME OF ROAD.	TOTAL PROJECTED MILEAGE	MILES BUILT IN					TOTAL MILEAGE COMPL'D, INCLUSIVE OF SIDINGS TO FEB. 1, 1876.
			1871.	1872.	1873.	1874.	1875.	
Massachusetts	Boston, Revere Beach and Lynn	9					9	9
"	Grafton	3				3		3
"	Martha's Vineyard	9				9		9
"	Worcester and Shrewsbury	6½			3			3
New York	Bath & Hammondsport	9½					9½	9½
"	Central Valley	24			12			12
"	Crown Point	13			13	2	1	16
"	Peekskill Valley	7			7			7
New Jersey	Camden, Gloucester & Mt. Ephraim	12			3		3	6
Pennsylvania	Bell's Gap	19			9			9
"	East Broad Top	30			11	19	5	35
"	Greenlick	6½					3½	3½
"	Lawrenceville & Evergreen	2¾			2¾			2¾
"	Mauch Chunk & Summit Hill	15				15		15
"	Montrose	27		14	11			25
"	Parker & Karns City	14			4	6		10
"	Peachbottom	60			8	30	7	55
"	Pittsburgh & Castle Shannon	45		3	3	4		10
"	Railway of Cambria Iron Co	25		25				25
"	Wapwollapen	6				6		6
Ohio	Cincinnati & Westwood	5					5	5
"	College Hill	3					3	3
"	Ohio and Toledo	65				22		22
"	Painesville and Youngstown	64		12	11	41	4	68
"	Toledo and Maumee	9				8		8
Indiana	St. Louis, Bloomfield & Louisville	66					6	10
Illinois	Cairo & St. Louis	146½		25	65	10	65	165

Narrow Gauge Railways in Operation (Continued.)

STATE OR TERRITORY.	NAME OF ROAD.	TOTAL PROJECTED MILEAGE.	MILES BUILT IN					TOTAL MILEAGE COMPL'D INCLUSIVE OF SIDINGS TO FEB. 1, 1876.
			1871.	1872.	1873.	1874.	1875.	
Illinois	Chicago, Millington & Western	200					12	12
"	Galena & Southern Wisconsin	72				30		20
"	Havana, Rantoul & Eastern	130					40	40
Iowa	Des Moines & Minnesota	197				37		37
"	Farmers' Union	300					12	20
"	Iowa Eastern	200		15	1	4	1½	21½
"	St. Louis, Keosauqua & St. Paul	230					4	4
Missouri	West End Narrow Gauge	16½					8	10
"	Wyandotte, Kansas City & N. W.	240				10	7	21
Kansas	Kansas Central	550		56				56
Colorado	Colorado Central	49		21	4			25
"	Denver & Rio Grande	850	76	87		9	2	210
"	Denver, South Park & Pacific	100				16		16
"	Golden City & South Platte	25			19			19
Utah	American Fork	21		18				18
"	Bingham Cañon	23			18	5		23
"	Summit County	9			9			9
"	Utah Northern	450		30	27	20	10	97
"	Utah Western	45				18	20	38
"	Wasatch & Jordan Valley	20				12	8	20
Nevada	Eureka & Palisade	90				50	50	100
"	Eureka and Ruby Hill	6					6	6
"	Lake Tahoe	8					8	8
"	Nevada Central	18			18			18
California	Almeda, Oakland & Piedmont	60			10			10
"	Monterey & Salinas Valley	35				19		19
"	Nevada County	22					14	19
"	North Pacific Coast	225				51	9	60
"	Santa Cruz	20				8	12	20

California	Santa Cruz & Felton	6					6	6
"	San Luis Obispo	36				9		9
"	Stockton & Ione	40					18	18
Washington	Olympia	20				20		20
"	Walla Walla	20				20		20
Michigan	Mineral Range	100			12½	1	½	14
Virginia	Longdale	6¾				6¾		6¾
West Virginia	Ceredo	28			12			12
"	Pennsboro & Harrisville	9					9	9
Kentucky	Louisville, Harrods Creek & Westport	28			5			5
Tennessee	Duck River Valley	15				5		5
"	Memphis & Raleigh	10			10			10
South Carolina	Chester & Lenoir	104				25	27	52
Georgia	Memphis Branch	17			5			5
"	North and South of Georgia	130			23			23
Alabama	Cherokee	8	8					8
"	Tuskegee	6	6					6
Mississippi,	Natchez, Jackson & Columbus	180			10			10
"	Nashville & Vicksburg	450				20		20
"	Ripley	26		26				26
Arkansas	Arkansas Central	150		48				48
"	Hot Springs Branch	25					25	25
Texas	Corpus Christi, San Diego & Rio Grande	135					30	30
"	Rio Grande	22		8	14			22
"	Texas Western	450					20	20
Canada	Toronto, Grey & Bruce	191	40	47	57	51		210
"	Toronto & Nipissing	230	49	15	24			88
New Brunswick	Aroostook	20					15	20
"	New Brunswick	170			52	48		100
"	Riviere du Loup	91				91		91
Prince Edwards Is	Prince Edwards Island	200			50	70	80	200
Quebec	Phillipsburg & Yamaska	100					10	10
		7973	179	450	555¼	818¾	585	2687

The late John Edgar Thomson, when conversing with a gentleman who was requesting his opinion on the narrow gauge question, stated, "that were he now building certain of the branch roads of that great highway, the Pennsylvania Railroad, (one now carrying annually 10,000,000 tons of freight,) he would make them 3 feet instead of 4 feet 8½ inch gauge."

After such an endorsement by so celebrated an engineer and financier, whose whole life had been devoted to the study of railroading in its several departments, and with the past few years as a basis to stand upon, we believe that narrow gauge railways will be "a power in the land," and that they will revolutionize certain districts in America, and whole countries in other parts of the world, and be the means of making fruitful the barren places.

In support of the statement just made, we produce two tables taken from an official report, showing by counties the progress of Colorado in population and wealth from 1870 to 1874. The counties in bold type are those through which the Denver and Rio Grande Railway runs. It will be seen that their development is trebled and quadrupled. The Denver and Rio Grande was begun in 1870.

POPULATION.

COUNTY.	CENSUS 1870.	CENSUS 1873.
Arapahoe	6,829	25,000
Bent	592	3,850
Boulder	1,939	5,325
Clear Creek	1,596	5,500
Conejos	2,504	3,800
Costilla	1,779	3,350
Douglas	1,388	3,100
El Paso	987	3,450
Fremont	1,064	3,300
Gilpin	5,490	7,500
Greenwood	510	600
Huerfano	2,250	3,350
Jefferson	1,390	6,230
Lake	522	875
Larimer	838	3,250
Las Animas	4,276	5,780
Park	447	2,800
Pueblo	2,265	**8,950**
Saguache	304	2,000
Summit	258	1,050
Weld	1,636	5,100
Totals	39,864	104,860

ASSESSMENT LIST.

COUNTY.	1870.	1874.
Arapahoe	$4,731,830	$15,088,085
Bent	351,248	2,172,267
Boulder	1,121,972	2,547,964
Clear Creek	1,100,112	1,485,008
Conejos, including La Plata	265,702	141,415
Costilla, including Rio Grande	118,062	528,249
Douglas	574,397	1,470,636
Elbert		1,675,760
El Paso	524,965	3,160,323
Fremont	375,950	1,314,695
Gilpin	2,000,000	2,322,342
Greenwood	446,924	Abolished in 1874.
Huerfano	324,932	702,856
Jefferson	1,034,738	2,034,529
Lake	172,917	250,998
Larimer	332,510	905,944
Las Animas	457,932	1,186,482
Park	175,550	795,707
Pueblo	857,811	3,784,348
Saguache	129,656	599,308
Summit	123,926	158,722
Weld	954,361	2,063,166
Totals	$16,015,521	$44,388,804

The Secretary of the Utah Western Railway writes: "The promoters of broad gauge roads here, as elsewhere, try to retard the narrow gauge as much as possible; but in spite of this the broad gauge has built only 87 miles since May 17, 1869, while there have been built about 200 miles of narrow gauge since August 23, 1871, with a very good prospect of making a grand union road during the coming summer, to unite most of the narrow gauge roads in Utah."

On a previous page the subject of converting broad gauge lines into narrow gauge railways, in certain instances, was briefly mentioned. It has been demonstrated that a narrow gauge railway will be remunerative where a broad gauge cannot, owing to its much larger expenditures; it is therefore not to be wondered at that the directors of such, being convinced of the efficiency and lesser expenditure of the narrow gauge railway, should convert their line into one by altering the gauge and disposing of the rolling stock for other, seeing that if this is not accomplished, their railway must be run at a loss, or else train service must be discontinued.   Or again, where certain short lines, built on the standard gauge, connect with trunk lines, built on the narrow gauge, and it is expedient to overcome break of gauge, and consequent transhipment, that such lines be converted into 3 feet ones; or further, where the surveys being made for a standard gauge, the original intention being to construct a line 4 feet 8½ inches wide, subsequent consideration on the probable traffic and consequent revenue, induced the construction of a narrow gauge railway.

The following railways are mentioned as an example of each proposition :

The Chester and Lenoir Narrow Gauge Railway, formerly the Kings Mountain Broad Gauge Railroad.

The San Rafael and San Quentin, leased by the North Pacific Coast Narrow Gauge Railway, and converted into one of 3 feet.

The Kalamazoo, Lowell and Northern Michigan Railway, organized for standard gauge, and to be constructed of narrow gauge.

Of the roads mentioned in the preceding table, the following have the amount of mileage set opposite each respectively under construction :

	MILES.
Worcester and Shrewsbury Extension	16
Camden, Gloucester, and Ephraim	6
Peachbottom	5
St. Louis, Bloomfield, and Louisville	60
Chicago, Millington and Western	100
Havana, Rantoul and Eastern	90
Farmers' Union	12
West End	7
Wyandotte, Kansas City, & N. W.	5
Denver and Rio Grande	50
Golden City and South Platte	2
Utah Northern	20
North Pacific Coast	25
San Luis Obispo	3
Chester and Lenoir	20
Texas Western	25

During 1876 a very large amount of narrow gauge mileage will be completed, as the railways in operation have fully demonstrated their capacity in every class of traffic, and their economical operation will induce capital to seek them as investments. · They should however be constructed from stock subscriptions, paid by the community along the route, and those interested in the development of the region, who are the interested parties in the operation of the railway. The most conservative financiers recommend that the whole cost of the road should be so divided between the stockholders and the bondholders that not more than one-fourth of the total amount should be raised by bonds, while three-fourths should be raised by stock subscriptions, aided by outside help. Floating debts should never be too heavy—at any sacrifice a new railroad should place its debt beyond contingencies. The late Chief Justice Chase, when Secretary of the Treasury, in 1861, laid down this principle in a striking form. It was essential, he said, for a large debtor to maintain control over his indebtedness. It is especially needful for railroads to get such control. And of the legitimate rules for doing so, the chief one is this: To avoid demand obligations, and to convert, as rapidly as possible, their floating debt into long bonds.

On the next page we give a list of the companies in the most forward state, that have been recently heard from; also their total projected mileage, and their mileage under construction, and the address to which communications should be sent, prefacing it with the remark that the data here given are as correct as circumstances will permit, seeing that there is no Bureau or organization created purely for the collection of such statistics, and to which narrow gauge railways could report. It is, therefore, not improbable that those lines that are reported as surveyed, may have their line graded, and those stated as under construction have part of their line ironed and in operation.

STATE OR TERRITORY.	NAME OF ROAD.	Projected Mileage.	Mileage Under Construction.	ADDRESS.
Massachusetts...	Bedford Branch	7	Organizing.	C. E. Mansfield, Boston.
"	Boston, Lawrence & Haverhill	30	Being surveyed.	Hon. James M. Carlton, Haverhill.
"	Green Mountain	225	"	Saml. Wells, Montpelier, Vt.
New Jersey	South New Jersey	16	"	Wm. S. Mattson, Woodstown.
Pennsylvania....	Waynesburg & Washington	28	28	J. G. Ritchie, Waynesburg.
"	Washington & Nineveh	18	Being surveyed.	R. W. Parkinson, Sparta.
Ohio	Dayton & Southeastern	115	115	J. Blickensderfer, C. E., Dayton.
"	Lake Erie, Alliance & Wheeling	150	30	Hugh Blakeley, Alliance.
"	Miami Valley	52	Being surveyed.	S. S. Haines, Prest., Waynesville.
"	Portsmouth & Pound Gap	520	Surveys made.	J. W. Fulton, Portsmouth.
"	Ravenna & Cleveland	40	Being surveyed.	Ofice at Cleveland.
"	Springfield, Jackson & Pomeroy	105	105	James Emmet, Prest., Waverly, Clarke Co.
"	Toledo & St. Louis		Being surveyed.	Geo. C. Chaffee, Pres.
Indiana	Brazil, Worthington & Bloomfield	45	"	P. McKissick, Prest., Brazil.
Illinois	Fond du Lac, Amboy & Peoria	220	"	Office at Fond du Lac.
"	Keithsburg & Eastern	250	86	J. K. Hornish, Prest, Keithsburg.
"	Peoria & Mississippi	90	Surveyed.	Office at Peoria.
"	Springfield & St. Louis	45	Graded.	A. Starne, Prest., Springfield.
Iowa	Ames & Eldora	35	Being surveyed.	Office at Ames.
"	Burlington & Northwestern	50	Being Graded.	— Cameron, C. E., Burlington.
Wisconsin	La Crosse & Viroqua	36	Being surveyed.	N. McKie, Prest., La Crosse.
"	Milwaukee and Southwest	300	40	J. H. Stearns, C. E., Milwaukee.
"	Tomah & Chicago	30	30	
Minnesota	Caledonia & Mississippi	24	12	Office at Caledonia.
"	Minneapolis & Northwestern	200	35 m. surveyed.	Geo. B. Wright, Minneapolis.
"	Wabasha & Faribault	70	40	W. S. Walton, Wabasha.
"	St. Cloud & St. Peter	96	20	J. P. Wilson, Prest., St Cloud·
Michigan	Kalamazoo, Lowell & Northern Michigan	68	68	G. E. Dunbar, Sec'y., Kalamazoo.
Missouri	St. Louis & Manchester	18	18	John F. Long, St Louis.
"	St. Louis & Western	300	Surveys made.	Chas. Hunt, St. Louis.
Kansas...	Walnut Valley	60	Being surveyed.	P. P. Plumb, Prest., Emporia.

State	Railroad	Miles	Status	Officer
California	California Central	175	Being graded.	Reuben Morton, Prest., San Francisco.
"	Santa Clara Valley	40	" "	Henry Bartling, Prest., San Jose.
"	San Francisco & San Mateo	80	36	L. H. Shortt, C. E , San Luis Obispo.
"	Sonoma & Marin	34	22	W. H. Knight, Sec'y., San Francisco.
Texas	Central Narrow Gauge	120	Being surveyed.	Wm. S. Herndon, Prest., Tyler.
"	Southwestern & Rio Grande	200	23 miles graded.	W. S. Haven, Prest, Shreveport, La.
Tennessee	Greenville & Paint Rock	22	8	O. G. Vanderhoof, C. E., Knoxville.
"	Memphis & Knoxville	350	35 miles graded.	Hon. John C. Brown, Pulaski.
Alabama	Florence & Tuscaloosa	100	Surveys made.	Office at Tuscaloosa.
South Carolina	Cheraw & Salisbury	51	28	B. D. Townsend, Society Hill.
"	Cheraw & Chester	95	29	Fleming Gardner, C. E., Chester.
Virginia	Elizabeth City & Norfolk	70	70	Office at Elizabeth City.
"	Richmond & Trans-Alleghany	250	Surveys made.	John Enders, Prest., Richmond.
"	Danville & New River	30	"	Hon. C. Y. Thomas, Martinsville.
"	Washington, St. Louis & Cincinnati	793	30	P. B. Borst, Prest., Luray.
Kentucky	Mt. Sterling	18	18	C. J. Glover, Mt. Sterling.
West Va.	New River	67	67	J. D. Sargeant, Prest., Philadelphia.

With but few exceptions, three feet between the rails has been the width adopted by the narrow gauge railways of the United States; this gauge being found the most servicable for carrying every variety of freight. Of the railways with a less gauge than three feet we must notice The Sumner Heights and Hazelwood Valley Railroad, of ten inch gauge—the narrowest gauge railroad in the world. This new departure is the idea of Mr. Geo. E. Mansfield, of Walpole, N. H., who projected and built it during 1875. The line is one-third of a mile in length, and starts from the summit of a small hill just back of the Hazelwood station, on the Providence Railroad, and after winding round the hill by sharp curves, comes down through his back yard, and by an apparently very dangerous curve shoots obliquely across one street, closely shaving a street corner where it runs over a small bridge, and then across another street to the side near the railroad, and thence for a short distance parallel with the latter. The ties or sleepers are composed of narrow strips of inch board about fifteen inches long, upon which are nailed (with small finish nails) rails made of soft wood, about an inch square and ten inches apart. On these are nailed narrow strips of thin hoop iron, and the whole affair is complete. The car used on this road is a platform, about two feet wide and five feet long, and the diameter of the wheels is five inches. It would seem, at first sight, that the whole affair was a mere boy's plaything, and a dangerous one at that; but a test of its capacity would soon undeceive the proprietor of such hasty judgment. It would appear, to begin with, that the wheels of the car, with their small flanges, would be sure to jump the track at every curve, but by a peculiarity in the way of connecting them with the car (an invention of Mr. Mansfield) they follow the track in every wind and curve as surely as if they were eighteen inches in diameter and had a corresponding depth of flange. The maximum grade is 715 feet to the mile, and the sharpest curvature 25 feet radius. There is one bridge sixty feet long on a curve and grade of 440 feet to the mile. Four heavy men can ride in the car, which descends by gravitation, and is under complete brake control; and those who have ridden upon it are surprised at the absence of oscillation.

Donkeys laden with narrow gauge rails for the Silverton Railroad on the main street of Silverton, Colorado, 1887

A front view and a cab view of this engine are reproduced as the frontispiece and tailpiece respectively in this book

NARROW GAUGE LOCOMOTIVES.

The locomotives for working narrow gauge railways necessarily conform to the same principles as those for the standard gauge; when, therefore, the projectors of the initial narrow gauge railway in the United States requested the Baldwin Locomotive Works of Philadelphia to submit designs for passenger and freight engines, their drawings did not essentially differ except in dimensions from those made for standard roads. A description of the first passenger engine, constructed in June, 1871, and aptly named "Montezuma," its mission being to run through the territories once owned by that ancient monarch, will not be out of place.

The engine has four drivers connected and a two-wheeled truck.

Diameter of cylinders, 9 inches.	Stroke of piston,	16 inches.
" " driving wheels, ...	40	"
" " pony wheels, ...	24	"
Distance between centre of pony wheels and centre of front drivers,	5ft.	8½ "
Distance between driving wheel centres, . . .	6	3 "
Total wheel base of engine, ...	11	11½ "
Rigid wheel base (distance between driving wheel centres), .	6	3 "
Diameter of tender wheels, ...	24	"
Distance between centres of tender wheels, . . .	6	"
Total wheel base of tender and engine, . . .	20	5½ "
Length of engine and tender over all, . . .	35	4 "
Capacity of tender, ...	500 gals.	
Weight of tender empty, ...	5,500 lbs.	
" " engine in working order, . . .	25,300	"
" " " on drivers, ...	20,500	"
" " " on each pair of drivers, . .	10,250	"
" " " on pony wheels, ...	4,800	"
Height of smoke stack above rail, ...	9	9 "
Height of cab from foot board to centre of ceiling, . .	6	3 "

Its tractive power, exclusive of the resistance of curves, is as follows :

On a level, ...	512 gross tons.	
On a grade of 40 feet to the mile, . . .	164	" "
On a grade of 80 feet to the mile, . . .	98	" "

From these figures should be deducted 17 gross tons, the weight of the engine and tender in working order, to get the total weight of cars and lading that can be drawn on a level or on the grades named. The speed attainable is between 25 and 35 miles per hour.

In the course of time defects were apparent in engines for passenger service constructed as above. Locomotives, therefore, are not now built on that pattern, but made similar to the "Baldwin," a view of which is given on opposite page.

The following is a description of an engine built by the National Locomotive Works at Connellsville, Pa.

This engine has four connected drivers and a four-wheeled truck.

Diameter of cylinders, 12 inches.	Stroke of piston, 18 inches.
" " driving wheels,	46 "
" " truck wheels,	22 "
Total wheel base,	18ft. "
Rigid wheel base,	6 8 "
Tender, eight-wheeled, tank capacity,	1,200 gals.
Diameter of tender wheels,	24 inches.
Distance between centres of tender wheels,	48 "
Total wheel base of engine and tender,	36ft. 8 "
Length of engine and tender over all,	43 3 "
Weight of tender empty,	11,600 lbs.
" " engine in working order,	37,000 "
" " " on drivers,	26,000 "
" " " on truck,	11,000 "
Height of smoke stack above rail,	11 feet
" " cab from foot board to centre of ceiling,	6 " 5 in.

TRACTIVE POWER.

On a level,	740 gross tons.
On a 20 foot grade,	395 " "
On a 40 foot grade,	260 " "
On a 60 foot grade,	195 " "
On a 80 foot grade,	140 " "
On a 100 foot grade,	115 " "

The following is a description of an eight-wheeled locomotive built by the Brooks Locomotive Works, of Dunkirk, N. Y.:

Diameter of cylinders, 11 inches.		Stroke of piston, 16 inches.
" " driving wheels,	. . . . .	44 "
" " truck wheels,	. . . . .	20 "
" " driving wheel centre,	. . . .	39½ "
Total wheel base of engine,	. . .	16ft. 1 "
Rigid wheel base,	. . . . . .	6 "
Diameter of tender wheels,	. . . . .	24 "
Total wheel base of engine and tender,	. . .	30 9 "
Capacity of tender,	. . . . . .	800 gals.
Weight of engine in working order,	. . . .	25,000 lbs.
" " " on drivers,	. . . .	17,000 "
" " " on leading truck,	. . . .	8,000 "

The boiler is of the kind known as wagon top style and made of Pennsylvania charcoal iron ¼ inch thick. Cylinder part of boiler 35 inches diameter at smoke box end; made telescoping back. Dome 22 inches diameter and 22 inches high, placed over fire box. Flues 82 in number, 1¾ inches diameter, 7 feet 6¼ inches long, set with copper bushing at fire-box end. Before lagging is put on, boiler to be fired up and tested as perfectly tight under a steam pressure of 155 pounds.

The fire box is of homogenous cast steel 49½ inches long and 18½ inches wide inside. Sides, crown and back sheets ¼ inch thick; flue sheets ⅜ inch thick. Water space 2½ inches back and sides, 2½ inches front. Stay bolts of Ulster iron ⅞ inches diameter, placed not over 4½ inches apart, screwed and riveted over sheets at both ends. Crown bars made of two bars iron 4 inches by ⅝ inch, welded at ends, placed not over 5½ inches from centre to centre; ends having firm bearing on side sheets. Crown sheet securely fastened to bars by rivets placed not over 4½x5½ inches apart. Grates adapted for the fuel ; ash pan, approved design ; smoke stack, adapted for the fuel.

Safety valves, two in number, patent relief valves placed in dome, one set to limit the pressure desired, the other adjustable by a lever in cab.

Frames, of hammered iron with pedestals welded on, planed full length. Top bar 2½x3 inches. Pedestals cased with cast iron gibs and wedges, to prevent wear by the boxes.

Pistons, to have cast iron spider and follower with Dunbar's patent steam packing, with rods of patent cold rolied iron.

Guides, of hammered iron case-hardened, 2½ inches wide, 1⅛ inches thick at each end and 1⅛ inches thick in the middle, fastened to yoke.

Valve motion, approved shifting link style, graduated to cut off equally at all points of the stroke. Links of best hammered iron well case-hardened. Rocker shafts of wrought iron with journals 2¾ inches diameter, and 8 inches long; arms ⅞ inches thick. Reverse shaft made with arms forged on.

Tyres, of best crucible cast steel, flanged, 5 inches wide, and 2¼ inches thick when finished.

Driving axles, of best hammered iron; journals 5 inches diameter, and 6 inches long. Wheel fit 5 inches diameter, 6 $\frac{3}{32}$ inches long.

Wrist pins, of best cast steel. Wheel fit 5⅞ inches long and 3¼ inches diameter. Main wrist 3 inches in diameter and 3 inches long. Side rod wrist 2½ inches in diameter and 2¼ inches long.

Springs, of best quality of cast steel.

Feed water, supplied by two brass pumps with valves and cages of brass, well fitted. Plungers of patent cold rolled iron: or one pump and one No. 5 injector. Cock in feed pipe regulated from foot-board.

Engine cab, to be substantially built of walnut well finished, and securely braced to boiler and running boards.

Pilot, to be made of oak and ash, well braced.

Finish—Boiler lagged with wood, jacketed with Russia iron secured by brass bands. Dome lagged with wood, with brass casing on body. Top and bottom ring of brass or iron. Cylinders lagged with wood, jacketed with brass, with brass casing heads. Steam chests cased with brass. Top cover to be made of cast iron. Cylinders oiled from cab by pipes under jacket.

Its tractive power, exclusive of the resistance of curves, in addition to weight of engine and tenders, is as follows :

On a level, ...	550 gross tons.
On a grade of 20 feet to the mile, ...	250 " "
On a grade of 40 feet to the mile, . . .	150 " "
On a grade of 60 feet to the mile, ...	100 " "
On a grade of 80 feet to the mile, ...	80 " "
On a grade of 100 feet to the mile, ...	70 " "

The next illustration is of a " Mogul" engine, built at the same works. This style of locomotive is recommended by Mr. Brooks in his letter to the author, which will be found at the end of the chapter.

With the exception of the following alterations, the specification for an eight-wheeled engine is suitable for the Mogul pattern.

Fire box 60 inches long, 18½ inches wide inside.

Diameter of cylinders, 11 inches.	Stroke of piston, 16 inches.
" " driving wheels, ...	36 "
" " truck wheels, ...	24 "
" " driving wheel centre, ...	32 "
Total wheel base of engine, ...	15ft. 9 "
Rigid wheel base, ...	10 6 "
Diameter of tender wheels, ...	24 "
Total wheel base of tender and engine, . . .	31 7 "
Capacity of tender tank, ...	1,000 gals.
Weight of engine in working order, . . .	33,000 lbs.
" " " on drivers, ...	28,000 "
" " " on truck wheels, . . .	5,000 "

Guides, of hammered iron case-hardened, 3 inches wide, 1⅛ inches thick at each end and 1⅛ inches thick in the middle, fastened to yoke.

Valve motion, approved shifting link style, graduated to cut off equally at all points of the stroke. Links of best hammered iron well case-hardened. Rocker shafts of wrought iron with journals 2½ inches diameter, and 10⅜ inches long; arms ⅞ inches thick. Reverse shaft made with arms forged on.

Driving wheels, 6 in number, 32 inches diameter inside of tyre. Centres of cast iron constructed with hollow hubs and rims, solid spokes, relieving the centres from all strain from contraction in cooling by a uniform distribution of metal.

Tyres, of best crucible cast steel, flanged, 5 inches wide, and 2 inches thick when finished. Tyres on middle pair of drivers plain, 5½ inches wide.

Driving axles, of best hammered iron; journals 5 inches diameter, and 6 inches long. Wheel fit 5 inches diameter, 6 $\frac{3}{32}$ inches long.

Wrist pins, of best cast steel. Wheel fit 6 inches long and 3½ inches diameter. Main wrist 3 inches in diameter and 2½ inches long. Side rod wrist 2½ inches in diameter and 2½ inches long.

Feed water, supplied by one brass pump outside of cross head, with valves and cages of brass, well fitted. Plungers of hollow tubing. One No. 5 injector. Cock in feed pipe regulated from foot-board.

Its tractive power, exclusive of the resistance of curves, is as follows:

On a level, ...	. 750 gross tons.
On a grade of 20 feet to the mile, ...	350 " "
On a grade of 40 feet to the mile, . . .	. 225 " "
On a grade of 60 feet to the mile, ...	150 " "
On a grade of 80 feet to the mile, . . .	. 125 " "
On a grade of 100 feet to the mile, ...	100 " "

The following letter from the President of the Brooks Locomotive Works to the author is of such interest that we produce it entire:

My Dear Sir:—Will you kindly allow me space in your

Consolidation type freight locomotive built for Denver & Rio Grande Railway. Built by Baldwin Locomotive Works. Cylinders, 14x16″. Drivers, 40″. Total weight, 52,000 pounds

Mogul type freight locomotive for the Cairo & St. Louis Railroad built by Baldwin Locomotive Works.
Cylinders, 13x16″. Drivers, 36″ Total weight, 46,000 pounds

valuable publication upon the Narrow Gauge Railway System, to give briefly my reasons for recommending the so-called "*Mogul*" locomotive for all general traffic upon such a line, either passenger or freight. The importance of rightly deciding this question cannot be over-estimated; and my firm conviction as to its bearing upon the economical operation of the system must be my apology for this article.

The elements of friction obtaining from the operation of any given width of gauge of track or lateral base line for the support and movement of the equipment thereon, may be very properly classed under three separate heads.

1st. In the decreased proportionate weight of equipment to paying load moved.

2d. In the frictions resulting from the conditions of the vertical lateral centre of gravity, and the angle of stability.

3d. In the frictions resulting from the conditions of the angle of impingement of the flanges of the wheels upon the rails.

The entire economies resulting in the operation of a narrow gauge railway, obtain from these three heads; and therefore no one interested in the construction or maintenance of a narrow gauge railway can afford to ignore the advantages to be derived from a careful study and analysis thereof. Many persons are seemingly so carried away with the positiveness of these resulting economies, without regard to conditions, that they seem to fully believe that one pound avoirdupois weighs less than sixteen ounces. Actual weight, unfortunately, possesses no less gravity upon a narrow than upon a broad gauge; and therefore *nearly all* economies in this direction must be obtained under the conditions of the 1st head.

I say "nearly all," as there is a percentage of gain even in moving the same weight upon a narrow gauge, provided proper attention is paid to the conditions of the 2d head, and a constant certain percentage of gain always, in moving the same weight upon a narrow gauge, under the conditions of the 3d head.

One of the most important questions for the consideration of parties designing to construct, equip or operate a narrow gauge railway, is to decide upon such a weight and design of locomotive, as shall secure to them all the advantages to be derived from the adoption of such gauge. The proper distribution of weight in order that the maximum weight upon any one point upon the rail may never exceed a given limit, and that limit so largely under the capacity of a light iron rail to receive without injury, as to be used many years without perceptible depreciation, should receive minute attention and consideration. Now I assert as the experience resulting from a careful study of this question, that upon a 35 ℔ rail, the weight upon a single point should never exceed three tons: and I also assert that if the weight is kept down to two and one-half tons upon a single point, the rail will only wear out from lateral abrasions, and will be practically indestructible from hammering and consequent lamination.

Upon this question of locomotive equipment, minute consideration should be given to the conditions under the 2d head.

There is a misapprehension of the law governing the lateral oscillations and abrasions, from which obtain the frictions under the 2d head.

The fact, that the philosophical law of all lateral oscillations of the rolling stock *in motion*, in the abrasions of the wheels upon the rails, determine that such abrasions *shall be upon curved lines or upon arcs described by radii, from the vertical lateral centre of gravity to the point of contact of the wheels upon the rail*, in so far as the conflicting force of gravity will admit, seems to be ignored; and it is taken for granted that with any given deflection in the base line or track, the same results would obtain as when such rolling stock were not under forward or backward motion.

Suppose a vertical deflection obtains at a point under the wheels of a car or locomotive at rest; the lateral force obtained would be precisely as to the angle of deflection; because the effect of such deflection would obtain positively and directly when received; and would be *decreased* in force and quantity precisely in proportion to the *increased* width of gauge, or much less upon a broad, than upon a narrow gauge, with the same vertical deflection in each case.

Three typical narrow-gauge locomotives. Top and bottom illustrations show locomotives built by Porter Bell & Company; center by Brooks Locomotive Works

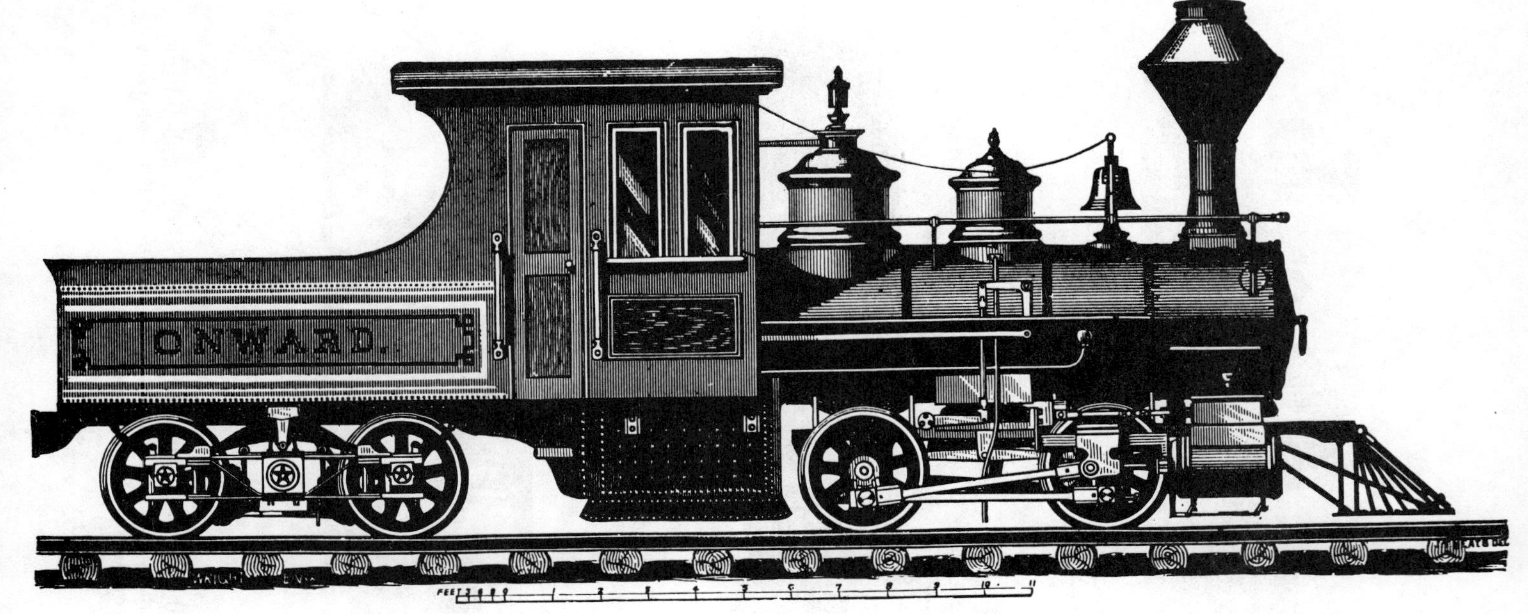

The first "Mason Bogie" type locomotive, built for the American Fork Railroad by Mason Machine Works, Taunton, Massachusetts

Whenever such car or locomotive is under motion, however, the *result* of any vertical deflection in the base line laterally, obtains far *beyond* the point where such deflection occurred; emanating directly from the centre of gravity of such moving body; and therefore the quantity of lateral abrasions and consequent friction resulting from any given deflection would be nearly as to the distance from the centre of gravity (vertical and lateral) to the point of contact of the wheels upon the rails.

Therefore, in order to secure the best results, a locomotive should be used having the minimum elevation of centre of gravity, and designed to give the most uniform steadiness of motion, as well as the most uniform distribution of weight.

I am aware that much prejudice exists against the "Mogul" locomotive for rates of speed exceeding 12 miles per hour, upon roads of standard gauge; and that the experience of railway managers invariably has been, that such a locomotive should only be used at slow rates of speed. There is no doubt that very heavy depreciation would follow the use of these locomotives at high rates of speed upon a standard gauge; for the reason that upon such gauge the lightest "Mogul" locomotive built has a weight upon each driving wheel exceeding five tons; and the general and more frequent fact is, that they are run with a weight exceeding *six* tons upon a single point. Now a weight even of five tons upon a single point upon an iron rail, is so very near the full capacity of resistance of such rail, that the added and consecutive blow of the extra driving wheel of the "Mogul" locomotive is a very large added element of depreciation; and hence the idea seems to obtain that the same difficulty would result from the use of the "Mogul" locomotive upon the narrow gauge for high rates of speed. This, however, is not the case where the maximum limit of weight upon a single point never exceeds *two and one-half tons;* for the reason that this weight is so largely under and within the capacity of an iron rail, that the added consecutive blow of the extra driving wheel is of no consequence; and the steadiness of motion attained by a properly proportioned and properly counterbalanced "Mogul" locomotive may be secured without fear of pernicious results.

There is not the slightest difficulty in attaining and maintaining a speed of *30 miles per hour* if desired, with a diameter of driving wheel thirty-six inches. A very high velocity is not expected nor generally desired upon the narrow gauge; and as the question of the elevation of the centre of gravity is really a most important one, driving wheels thirty-six inches in diameter will be found to give the best results in the end. Hence I do not hesitate to recommend a properly proportioned "*Mogul*" locomotive with thirty-six inch driving wheels, as the best and most economical for adoption for general traffic upon a narrow gauge.

There will be exceptions to this in the way of requirements for special service in the vicinity of large towns, where a light and frequent suburban passenger traffic exists; in which case a locomotive specially adapted to the specific service required, and not at all suited to general work, would be found to be the most serviceable.

Upon page 43 will be found a cut and general specifications of the Brooks Mogul three feet gauge locomotive; and while we desire to give our friends and patrons who favor us with orders such locomotives as *they* deem best in each special case, we take the liberty of recommending the "Mogul" locomotive as likely to give them the best satisfaction and the most satisfactory results.

Upon page 41 will be found cut and general specification of the standard eight wheel locomotive adapted to the narrow gauge.

Most respectfully submitted to yourself and your readers by

H. G. BROOKS,
Prest. Brooks Locomotive Works.

DOUBLE-TRUCK LOCOMOTIVE FOR DENVER, SOUTH PARK & PACIFIC (3-ft. Gauge) RAILROAD.

By Mason Machine Works, Taunton, Mass.

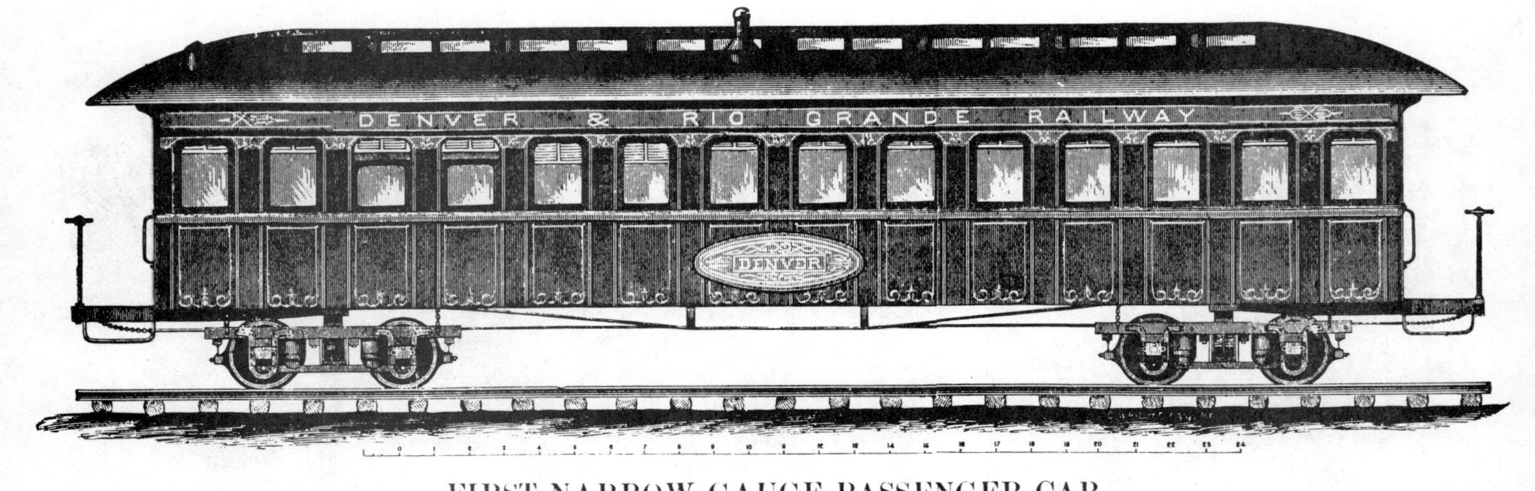

FIRST NARROW GAUGE PASSENGER CAR,

BUILT BY THE JACKSON & SHARP COMPANY,

WILMINGTON, DELAWARE,

1871.

NARROW GAUGE PASSENGER CARS.

When the question was first discussed of building Narrow Gauge Railways in the United States, the projectors naturally looked to the engineering fraternity of Great Britain for precedents. The result was apparent in the establishment of a measure of favor towards the use of four-wheeled passenger cars, built on the *coupé* plan, so common on European roads. Further reflection, however, decided that it would be impossible to revive a custom that had become so obsolete in America, as the one of confining a small number of passengers in the equivalent of a stage-coach body.

In the meantime the Jackson and Sharp Company, of Wilmington, Delaware, prepared and submitted designs for passenger cars, built on the American plan, of placing a long body on swinging trucks, to the Denver and Rio Grande Railway, the initial narrow gauge railway in the United States. These were approved and adopted by the managers, and on the opposite page will be seen a side view of the car "Denver," constructed in 1871, and being the first narrow gauge car built in America. The dimensions are as follows:

Length	. . . .	35 feet.	Weight . . .	15,000 pounds.
Width	. . . .	7 "	Dead wt. per pass. .	416 "
Height	. . .	10½ "	Capacity . . .	36 pass.
Diam. of wheel	. .	2 "	Ht. of sill from ground	27 inches.

The interior arrangement may be inferred from the accompanying cut. The seats are double on one side and single on the other, this arrangement being reversed in the centre of the car, so that each side carries half double and half single seats—an arrangement which secures a perfect balance of weight when the car is full.

The single seats are nineteen inches wide, the double seat, thirty-six inches, the aisle seventeen inches. These cars are finished in the best style; the wood work, the upholstery,

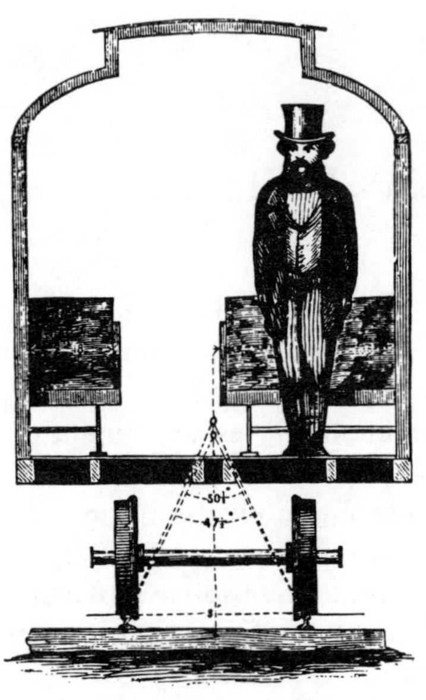

decorations, and the whole arrangement being first-class. The accompanying section shows how the angle of stability diminishes from fifty and one-half degrees for the empty car to forty-seven and one-half degrees for one loaded. This excellent result is due to a careful study of the parts, so that the load is carried within the shortest possible distance from the track. Even when exposed to the fierce onset of the Colorado gales, the cars have always proved themselves equal to the emergency. This has not been peculiar to that locality alone, but from all roads throughout the country the same satisfactory record has been received.

It was thought among narrow gauge engineers, when the system was in its infancy, that in no case should the width of car exceed double the gauge of the road. Even the seven feet width of body in the Denver and Rio Grande cars was regarded with feelings of apprehension until such time as the practical demonstration of the case proved the fallacy of the hypothesis. Since 1871 the width of cars has been steadily increased by builders, until at length a width of 8 feet over body has been attained and operated with great success. The height of cars has remained unaltered, and other details the same. A most important advantage has been secured by the change in width, for by this means it is possible to seat four passengers abreast instead of three, and thus increase the carrying capacity of the car from thirty-six to forty-seven passengers. This improvement especially commends itself to the wants of short lines of twenty to forty miles in length, and to temperate climates. In tropical climates it is best to keep the

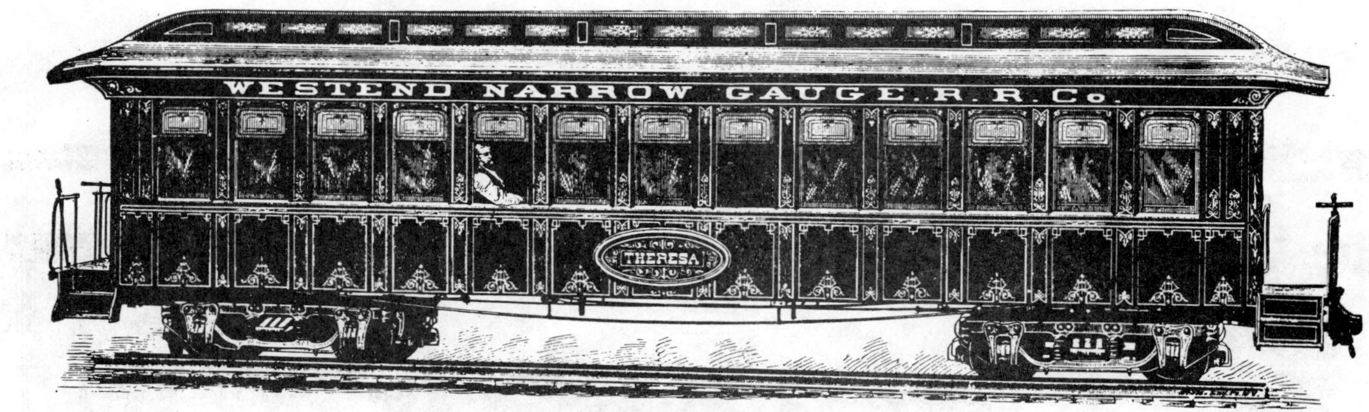

Narrow Gauge Passenger Car,

BUILT BY BARNEY & SMITH MANUFACTURING CO.,

DAYTON, OHIO.

35 ft. over sills, double seat each side of aisle, seats 46 Passengers, leaving room for stove and saloon. Weight 9¼ tons. Special notice asked to height of opening in window, giving ample room for Passengers to look out, and giving unusual opportunity for free ventilation through the large opening. All sash in deck made to open, a most important feature in so small a car with so great a carrying capacity.

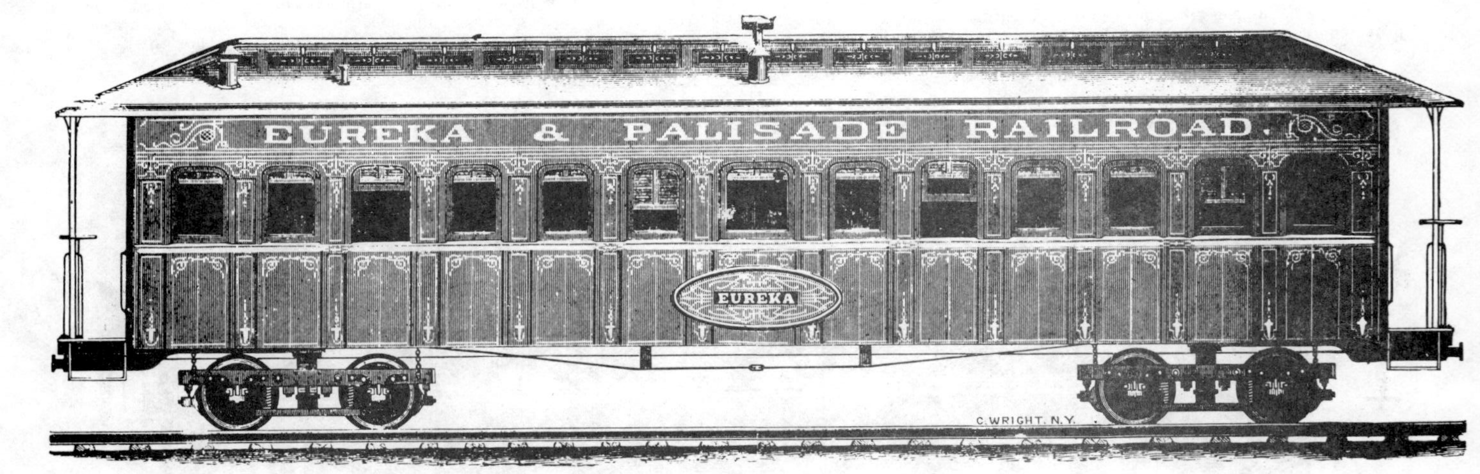

Narrow Gauge Passenger Car.

BUILT BY BILLMEYER & SMALLS,

YORK, PENN'A.

width at eight feet and lengthen the seats, so that three passengers will be accomodated abreast. Cars eight feet in width and seating four passengers abreast have an aisle of seventeen and one-fourth inches wide, and seat rooms of thirty-five inches each. As such cars weigh about 16,000 pounds, the dead weight per passenger is only 340 pounds. The saving in dead weight is very marked as compared with that of 722 pounds per passenger, so common on roads having a gauge of 4 feet 8½ inches.

Thus far we have described only the mode of seating the passengers in first-class cars in which the seats have reversible backs. In second- and third-class cars it is the custom of some builders to arrange the seats parallel to the walls of the car, the same way as obtains on street railways, and placing at the same time seats in the aisle for twelve passengers. The latter seats are arranged transversely and back to back. Where no saloon is used a car of thirty-five feet in length will seat, by this arrangement, sixty passengers, giving a dead weight of about 266 pounds per passenger. We leave it to others to infer what saving may safely be relied upon under such favorable relations between dead weight and effective load.

It can scarcely be necessary to enlarge on the comfort and ease enjoyed in the cars of the narrow gauge system, or to point out the close similarity in arrangement of stoves, saloons, sashes, ventilators, etc., common to the broad and narrow gauge systems. Suffice it to say that the Company who first demonstrated the feasibility of building comfortable passenger cars, has since manufactured most luxurious parlor as well as sleeping cars for roads of three feet gauge. There is, in fact, no limit to the comfort that can be secured with the development of the system.

The annexed cut represents a narrow gauge passenger car built for the "Eureka and Palisade Railroad Company," by Messrs. Billmeyer & Smalls. It is a first-class car, which for strength, beauty and comfort is not surpassed by any passenger car manufactured in this country. This car, named "Eureka," has a length of thirty-five feet in the body and forty-one feet out to out, and is seven feet in width, with a comfortable carrying capacity of thirty-six passengers; it weighs about 17,000 pounds, but could be built lighter without lessening much of its strength by the use of canvass instead of tin roofing, and by reducing the sizes of the irons and timbers used in its construction, though it is deemed by the builders of the "Eureka" far more important to guard against possible contingencies, than to save a few thousand pounds in the weight of the car.

The trucks are built of the best material and are after the most approved plans, securing to them strength and stiffness, and to the car the steadiness and easy motion always so desirable to travelers. The body of the car, which in design is similiar to the first-class coaches used on the Pennsylvania Railroad, is a model of strength and beauty, and is evidence of the superior artistic, as well as mechanical skill of its builders. Its frame work is of the best Southern Yellow Pine, braced and strengthened and put together in such manner as to secure the most perfect protection against accidents and at the same time give symmetry and grace to the appearance of the car when finished. The finest quality of poplar is used on the outside, while the richest and best varieties of hard wood, such as cherry, walnut and ash, are used with well selected profusion on the inside, and with its cushions of scarlet and green, and its hooks and lamps, and knobs, hinges, etc., of silver mounting give it the appearance of some fairy boudoir rather than a temporary convenience for the traveling public.

The coloring is all very fine, and though not gaudy, it is yet bound to attract and please the dullest lover of the beautiful.

A patent heating stove ornaments, and is at the same time of sufficient capacity to make the car comfortable in the coldest weather.

The Messrs. Billmeyer and Smalls in the "Eureka" have thus added to their reputation of long standing as among the best freight car builders in the United States, the title of first-class narrow gauge passenger coach builders.

They are now building for the Denver & Rio Grande R. R. Co. a number of first-class coaches, eight feet wide, forty-one feet total length, containing fourteen windows on each side,

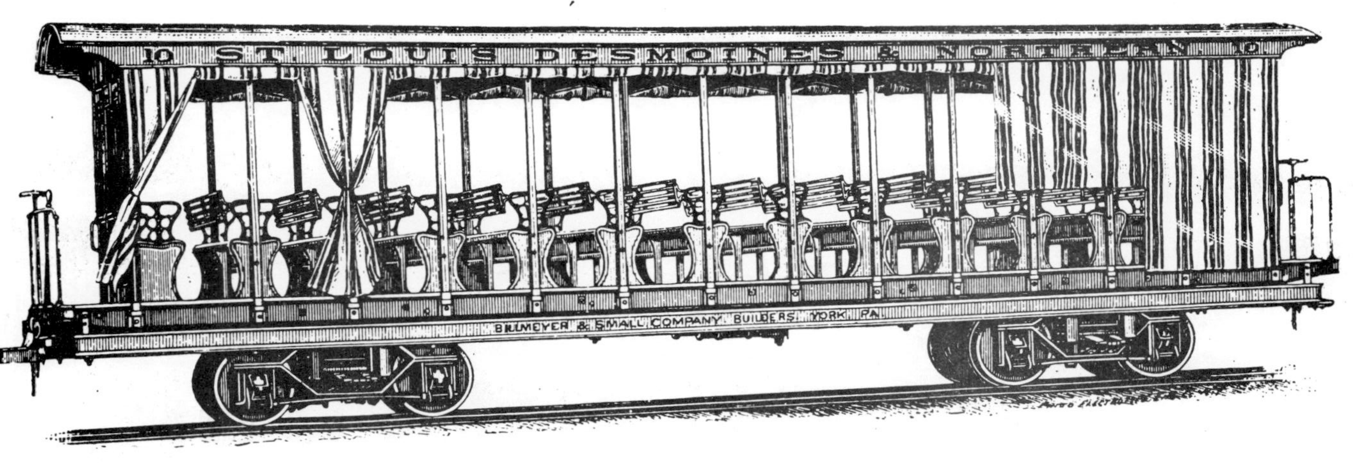

Excursion Car for the St. Louis, Des Moines and Northern Railway

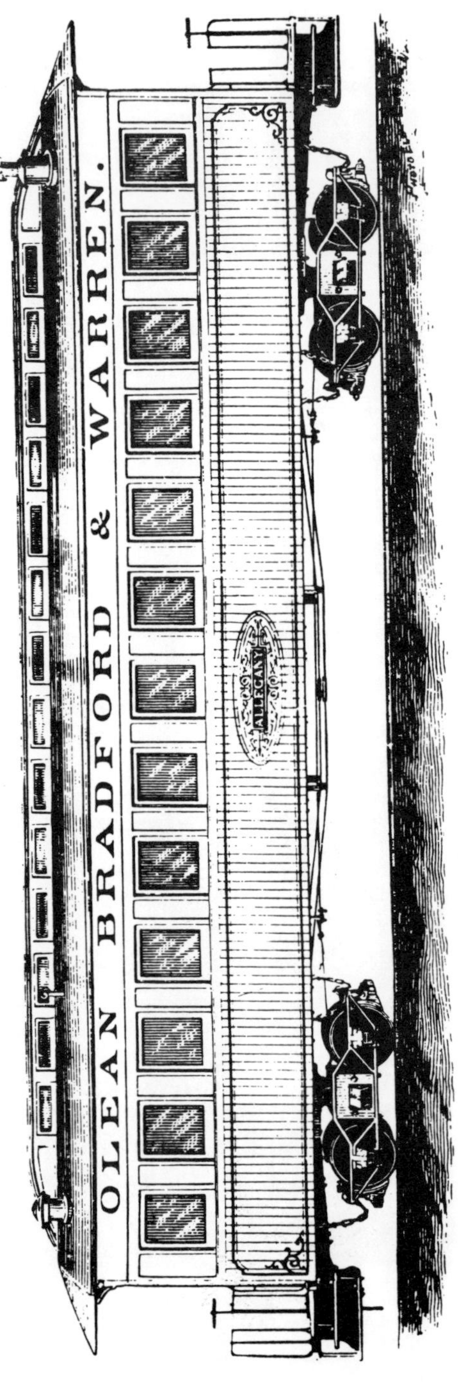

Passenger Car "Allegany" of the Olean, Bradford & Warren Railway

with two in each end of car, with twenty-five double seats, twelve on each side placed opposite each other and crosswise of the car, the other one placed at the end of the car back of the door, lengthwise of the car; with Miller platform and coupler, twenty-four inch wheels, etc.

By a vote taken at the Narrow Gauge Convention held in the City of St. Louis, June, 1872, it was decided that, as a matter of expediency, the height of the centre of drawheads of cars should be 24 inches above the upper surface of the rails. The wisdom of this cannot be overestimated, for with a three feet gauge there is no possible reason for a difference in height of drawheads on converging lines of road. If the 24-inch wheel is universally adopted as the standard, both in the case of passenger and freight service, then the narrow gauge system will have the uniformity of design recently established on the broad gauge. In the former case the height of drawhead would be 24 inches, and the diameter of the wheels 24 inches; in the latter 33 inches height of drawhead, and 33 inches standard height of wheel. Such dimensions are in accordance with the laws of most perfect stability for the freight, as well as the passenger cars.

The many improvements that have been adopted on the standard gauge, such as the Miller Platform and Coupler, the Westinghouse Air Brake, etc., have also been applied to narrow gauge cars with equal success; so that in mechanical as well as in artistic adaptability the narrow gauge system is equally pliable with the standard gauge, while in working economy it is vastly its superior.

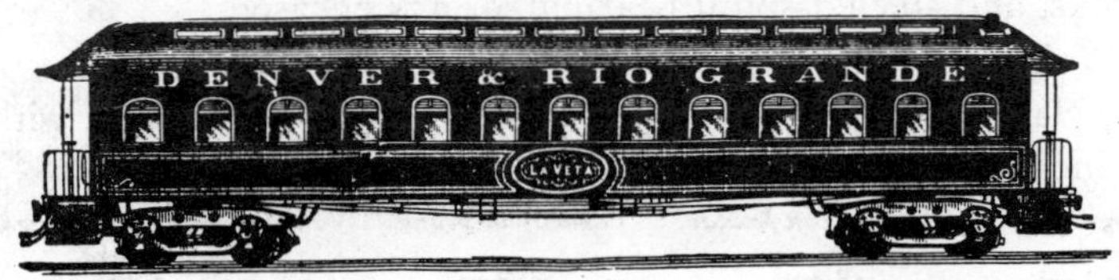

NARROW GAUGE FREIGHT CARS.

THE question as to whether narrow gauge freight cars could transport with equal facility the same class of freight as that carried in standard gauge cars, so naturally arose when railways of three feet gauge were projected, that it will not be inopportune to refer in this place to each class of car constructed, and compare it and its relative capacity with the same class on an ordinary gauge railway.

In 1871, the well-known car builders, Messrs. Billmeyer & Smalls, of York, Pa., were requested by the Denver and Rio Grande Railway Company to submit designs and dimensions for a Flat Car and Box Car, for their three feet gauge railway, then being constructed. The designs being approved, they commenced building *the first eight-wheeled narrow gauge freight car constructed in America.* A view and description of this car is given below:

Length of frame 23½ feet. Width, 6 feet. Wheels 20 inches in diameter, fitted on 3⅛ inch axles with steeled iron trucks, and steeled spiral bearing springs encased.

Weight of car, 6,250 pounds. Capacity, 10 tons. Cars of this class have been built 25 feet long, 6½ to 7 feet wide, with 24 inch wheels, and weighing about 7,500 pounds.

Gauge.	Weight of car in pounds.	Capacity in pounds.	Proportion of dead weight to paying load.
Standard	18,000	20,000	1 to 1.11
Narrow	6,250	19,000	1 to 3.04

The following is a view and description of the first eight-wheeled Box Car built by the same builders:

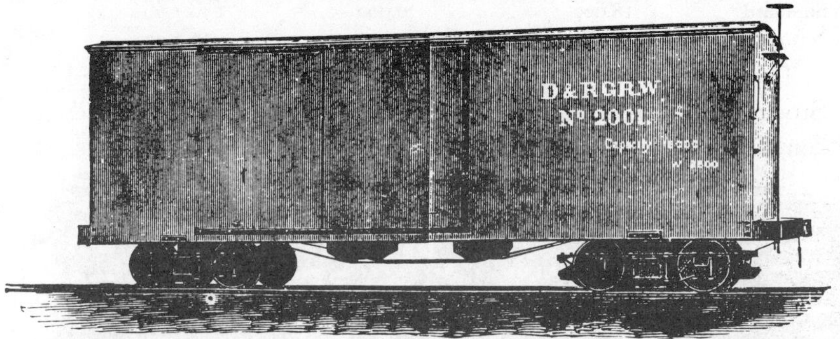

Length of frame, 23½ feet. Width, 6 feet. Wheels, 20 inches in diameter, fitted on 3⅛ inch axles, with steeled iron trucks, and steeled spiral bearing springs encased.

Weight of car 8,800 pounds. Capacity, 9 tons. Cars of this class are now being built 25 feet long, 7 feet wide, with 24 inch wheels, and weighing about 10,000 pounds.

Gauge.	Weight of car in pounds.	Capacity in pounds.	Proportion of dead weight to paying load.
Standard	19,000	20,000	1 to 1.05
Narrow	8,800	17,600	1 to 2

The following is a view and description of an eight-wheeled Coal Car with two drops in centre, designed and constructed by Messrs. Billmeyer & Smalls, for the East Broad Top Railway Company.

Length of frame, 23½ feet. Width, 6 feet. Wheels, 20 inches in diameter, fitted on 3⅛ inch axles with steeled iron trucks, and steeled spiral bearing springs encased.

Weight of car, 9,000. Capacity, 10 tons.

Gauge.	Weight of car in pounds.	Capacity in pounds.	Proportion of dead weight to paying load.
Standard .	18,000	30,000	1 to 1.66
Narrow . .	9,000	20,000	1 to 2.22

The following is a view and description of an eight-wheeled Stock Car, designed and constructed by Messrs. Billmeyer & Smalls, for the Costa Rica Railroad.

Length of frame, 23⅓ feet. Width, 7 feet. Wheels, 20 inches in diameter, fitted on 3⅛ inch axles with steeled iron trucks, and steeled spiral bearing springs encased.

Weight of car, 8,000 pounds. Capacity, 9 to 12 large head of cattle facing the ends of car, or 16 small cattle facing side of car.

Gauge.	Weight of car in pounds.	No. of cattle per car.	Weight of cattle in pounds.	Gross weight of loaded cars.	Total weight per head.
Standard,	18,000	14	19,600	37,600	1,285.
Narrow,	8,000	9	12,600	20,600	888.

Dead weight in favor of narrow gauge, 397.

A difference of 397 pounds per head, 3,573 pounds per car load of nine head, and in a train of twenty cars 71,460 pounds, or thirty-five tons in favor of the narrow gauge. Prominent stock men state that they prefer sending their stock to market in such cars, because the cattle steady themselves better, and there is less danger of their getting down, and because it is easier to feed and attend to them.

From the foregoing comparisons it will be seen that the least dead weight is hauled when a narrow gauge car is moved,

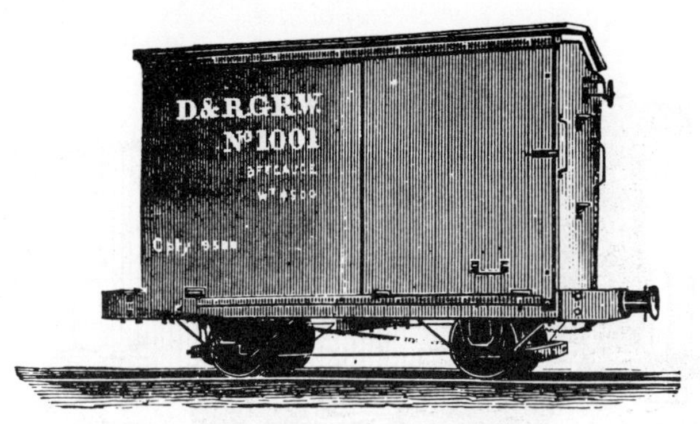

FOUR-WHEEL BOX CAR.

FOUR-WHEEL FLAT CAR.

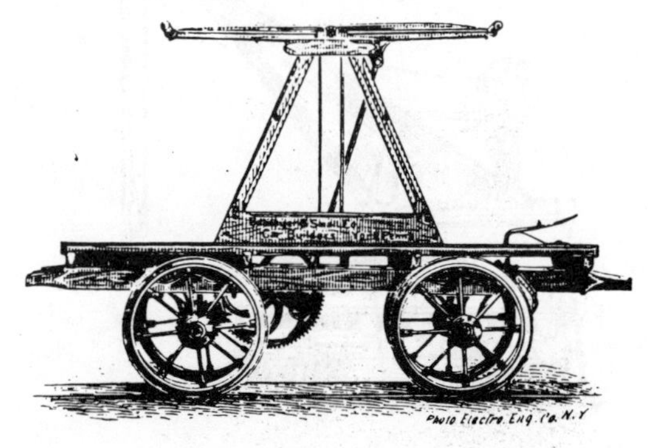

FOUR-WHEEL "DENVER" HAND CAR.

FOUR-WHEEL CABOOSE CAR.

FOUR-WHEEL COAL AND ORE CAR.

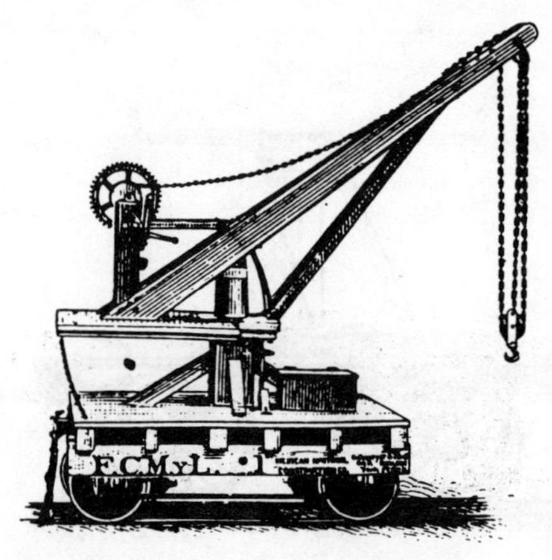

FOUR-WHEEL DERRICK CAR.

and that relatively a greater amount of paying weight is transported in it than in the standard gauge. This is one of its greatest advantages, and is well worth remembering. The following extract from the First Annual Report of the Denver and Rio Grande Railway Company is so much to the point, that we shall conclude this chapter with it:

With concentrated or heavy freight, which constitutes on this, as on nearly all railroads, the great bulk of the tonnage to be transported, the advantage realized has been 35 per cent. That it is to say, thirty-five hundredths more freight has been regularly carried on the narrow gauge rolling stock, with the same total weight of cars and load, as on the broad gauge. This can be most readily seen by observing a train of 16 loaded cars (which weigh say 8½ tons each when empty) arriving at Denver on the broad gauge road, and their contents transferred to the Denver and Rio Grande Railway. The *same freight* is placed in 20 narrow gauge cars, the empty weight of which is somewhat less than three tons each. The comparison will then stand as follows :

Cars.	Empty weight.	Paying load.	Total dead weight.	Total paying load.	Total weight cars and load.
16 wide-gauge	8½ tons each.	10 tons each.	136 tons.	160	296
20 narrow-gauge	less than 3 tons each.	8 "	60 "	160	220

Saving in total weight, 76 tons.

which is equivalent, after allowing for the weight of cars necessary to carry it, to 56 tons *additional freight* which the narrow gauge train could take without any increase of weight over the broad gauge train—in other words, 35 per cent. more; this is on the presumption that the cars on each gauge are fully loaded. But it very frequently happens in the ordinary course of railroad business that cars are not loaded to their capacity, in which event the narrow gauge receives a proportionately greater benefit. For instance, if from any station there was a load of but 5½ tons to carry, the narrow gauge car would weigh no more with this load than the broad gauge would entirely empty.

It is the case with almost any kind of freight that *whatever a car on the Denver and Rio Grande Railway holds of goods up to 5½ tons, is so much clear gain to it.* That is, it can carry that much in each car as cheaply as the wide gauge road can run its cars empty.

REPORTS OF ROADS.

ALAMEDA, OAKLAND AND PIEDMONT RAILROAD.

THIS Company was organized in February, 1873, to construct a narrow gauge railway from Oakland, in Alameda county, to Piedmont Hotel, a watering place on the Coast Range, thence into Contra Costa county, a distance of about 60 miles. During 1873, some ten miles were constructed between Oakland and Piedmont Hotel, that are reported to be doing a good business, as the line runs through a fine agricultural country.

No statistical information could be obtained.

The capital stock is $100,000, all paid in.

The office of the Company is at Oakland, Cal.

AMERICAN FORK RAILROAD.

This Company was incorporated on the 3d of April, 1872, to construct a narrow gauge railway from American Fork, a station on the Utah Southern Railroad, eastward, up the cañon, and passing the Miller and other mines, to Sultana, an estimated distance of 22 miles. Work was commenced in May, and by October, 18 miles were completed between the junction with the Utah Southern Railroad and the mines at the head of American Fork Cañon.

The maximum grade is 297 feet to the mile, and the average grade exceptionally heavy.

The sharpest curvature is 25° (299 feet radius).

The weight of rail is 30 pounds to the yard.

The weight of one of their engines, built by Messrs. Porter, Bell & Co., of Pittsburg, is 17 tons, having cylinders 12x16 and six drivers. This engine takes a train of over 47 tons up the maximum grade.

Financial statement—Capital stock authorized, $300,000; all paid in. No funded debt.

Lloyd Aspinwall, President, New York City.

H. Horner, Secretary and Treasurer, Salt Lake City.

E. Wilkes, Superintendent, Salt Lake City.

ARKANSAS CENTRAL RAILROAD.

This Company was organized in 1870 under the General Railroad Law of 1868, to build a railway of 3 ft. 6 in. gauge from Helena to Little Rock, a distance of 150 miles. During 1872, 48 miles between Helena and Clarendon were constructed and put in operation, and 80 miles graded, bridged and tied. Negotiations are on foot to procure money for the completion of the line.

The maximum grade is 52.8 feet to the mile.

The sharpest curvature is 13° 30' (425.40 feet radius).

The weight of rail 35 and 45 pounds to the yard.

The weight of engines, 8, 10 and 20 tons, all placed over the drivers.

Equipment—3 locomotives, 2 passenger cars, 1 baggage, 34 freight cars of all classes.

A. H. Johnson, President, Helena, Arkansas.

Edward Vernon, Vice-President, New York City.

J. A. Toppan, Superintendent, Helena, Arkansas.

BATH AND HAMMONDSPORT RAILROAD.

This company was incorporated by the Legislature of New York in 1872, to build a narrow gauge railway from Bath, on the Rochester division of the Erie Railway, northeastward through Pleasant Valley, to Hammondsport, at the foot of Crooked Lake, a distance of 9½ miles, and it is proposed to extend the line westward 20 miles to Hornellsville. Grading was commenced in 1872 and completed the following year, but track was not ironed till 1875.

The maximum grade is 132 feet to the mile, maintained for 6,000 feet, and the proportion of grade to level in entire line is as 9 to 10.

The sharpest curvature is 8° (717 feet radius), and the proportion of curvature to tangent in entire line two-ninths.

No. of bridges, 10; aggregate length, 1,000 feet.

No. of trestles, 1; aggregate length, 150 feet.

The weight of rail is 40 pounds to the yard.

Weight of engine 16½ tons, 13 tons on drivers.

Average cost of road per mile, including equipment, $13,000.

Equipment—2 locomotives, 2 passenger cars, 2 baggage and express, 4 freight cars.

Operations—Line only opened six months.

Financial Statement—Capital stock authorized, $100,000; paid in, $70,000; funded debt, 1st mortgage, $38,000; interest, 7%; floating debt, $5,000.

Allen Wood, lessee, Bath, N. Y.

N. W. Bennett, Superintendent, Bath, N. Y.

J. W. Davis, Secretary, Bath, N. Y.

BELL'S GAP RAILROAD.

This company was incorporated under the general law of Pennsylvania, May 11, 1871, with power to construct a railway from Bell's Mills, on the Pennsylvania Railroad, to Lloyds, in Cambria county, a distance of 8½ miles. The road has since been projected to Fallen Timber, making the total length 19 miles. The road was put under construction in 1872; and in June, 1873, 8½ miles were placed in operation. No additional mileage has since been added.

The grade is very heavy, the maximum of 158.4 feet to the mile being continuous for 6¾ miles.

The sharpest curvature is 28° (206 feet radius). There are ten of these curves on the maximum grade, two of which are 600 feet long, turning an angle of 168°.

The weight of rail is 35 pounds to the yard.

The weight of engines 15 tons.

Equipment—2 locomotives, 2 passenger cars, 78 freight cars of all classes.

Operations for year ending December 31, 1875—Gross earnings, $38,146.42. Operating expenses, $18,504.85 (48.49 per cent.). Net earnings, $19,641.57.

Financial statement—Capital stock authorized, $200,000; paid in, $200,000; funded debt, 1st mortgage, 7 per cent. bonds, maturing July 1, 1893, $200,000; floating debt, $8,800.

A. L. Massey, President, 11 Merchants' Exchange, Phila.
J. G. Cassatt, Secretary and Treasurer, Altoona, Pa.
Jos. Ramsary, Jr., Superintendent, Antestown, Pa.

BINGHAM CANON RAILROAD.

This company was organized in 1872, to build a narrow gauge railway from the mines at Bingham Cañon to Sandy Station, on the Utah Southern Railway, an estimated distance of 22 miles. Work was commenced in 1873, and 16 miles completed and put in operation between Sandy and the Winamuck Smelting Works. The following year the line was extended to Bingham Station and the Utah Mining Company's works, 6 miles.

The maximum grade is 240 feet to the mile. There is also a grade of 200 feet per mile, continuous for 3 miles, and the average grade is very heavy.

The weight of rail is 35 pounds to the yard.

The weight of engines 18 tons.

Cost of road, with equipment, per mile, $13,000.

Equipment—3 locomotives, 4 passenger cars, 1 baggage, 100 freight cars of all classes.

Operations for eleven months, ending October 31, 1874— Gross earnings, $103,247.39. Operating expenses, $40,711.76 (39.43 per cent). Net earnings, $62,535.63.

Financial statement—Capital stock authorized, $300,000; paid in, $45,000; funded debt, $240,000.

C. W. Scofield, President, New York City.
Geo. Goss, Vice-President, Salt Lake City.
George Doane, Secretary, Salt Lake City.

BOSTON, REVERE BEACH AND LYNN RAILROAD.

This company was incorporated under the railroad law of Massachusetts, May 23, 1874, to construct a narrow gauge railway between Boston and Lynn, a distance of 9 miles, which was commenced and built during 1875.

The maximum grade is 63½ feet to the mile, maintained for 300 feet, and the proportion of grade to level in entire line is one-tenth.

The sharpest curvature is 29° 23' (195 feet radius).

No. of tunnels, 1; aggregate length 500 feet.

No. of bridges, 13; aggregate length, 7,542 feet.

The weight of rail is 40 pounds to the yard.

Weight of engine 22 tons, twelve tons on drivers.

Average cost of road per mile, including equipment, $40,000.

Equipment—3 locomotives, 7 passenger cars, 8 freight cars.

Operations—The road has been running but six months, and so far very satisfactorily, and has earned about six per cent. net on the investment. Full report wlll be made at end of a year.

Financial statement—Capital stock authorized, $350,000; paid in, $347,600. No debt.

A. P. Blake, President, Boston.

John G. Webster, Treasurer, Boston.

Henry Breed, Superintendent, Boston.

CAIRO AND ST. LOUIS RAILROAD.

This company was organized in 1865, and a charter incorporating it passed February 16th, authorizing it to construct a railroad between St. Louis and Cairo, a distance of 146½ miles. In 1867 the charter was amended, but nothing was done until 1871, when it was resolved to build the line on a three feet gauge. The surveyed route of the road passes through the fertile counties of St. Clair, Monroe, Randolph, Jackson, Union and Alexander, touching at the towns of Columbia, Waterloo, Red-bud, Sparta, Murphysboro and Jonesboro. It passes through the finest fruit-growing district of Illinois and by the Chester and Big Muddy coal fields, and through large tracts of timbered land, much of which is yet to be cultivated. The first ground was broken August 30, 1871, and during 1872 thirty miles were operated. The following year 62 miles were constructed, bringing the line to Murphysboro. In 1874 twenty-six miles were built northward from Cairo, leaving a gap of thirty-two miles to be ironed during 1875, which is now laid.

The maximum grade is 104 feet to the mile, maintained for 4 miles, and the proportion of grade to level in entire line is 20%.

The sharpest curvature is 15° (383 feet radius), and the proportion of curvature to tangent of entire line is 10%.

No. of tunnels, 1; length 500 feet.

No. of bridges, 12; aggregate length, 3,960 feet.

No. of trestles, 26; aggregate length, 3 miles.

The weight of rail is 40 to 56 pounds to the yard.

Average weight of engines 19 tons, 15 tons on drivers.

Equipment—23 locomotives, 12 passenger cars, 3 baggage and express, 450 freight cars.

Cost of road, operations and financial statement are not reported.

H. R. Payson, President, St. Louis.

F. E. Canda, Vice-President, St. Louis.

J. L. Hinckley, General Supt., St. Louis.

CENTRAL VALLEY RAILROAD.

This company was incorporated by the Legislature of New York to build a narrow gauge railway between Bainbridge, a station on the Albany and Susquehanna Railroad, and Smithville Flats, Chenango county, N. Y., a distance of 12 miles. Construction commenced in 1872, and the line was opened for traffic the following year. It is purposed to extend it to McDonough, 12 miles further.

Efforts to obtain statistical information from this road have been without result.

Passenger cars were built for it by Messrs, Jackson & Sharp, of Wilmington, and freight cars by Messrs. Billmeyer & Smalls, of York, Pa.

H. S. Crozier, President, Smithville Flats, N. Y.

Thomas Hurley, Contractor, Smithville Flats, N. Y.

CHESTER & LENOIR RAILROAD.

This company was organized at Newton, N. C., on the 10th of July, 1873, to build a narrow gauge railway from Chester, S. C., to Lenoir, N. C., a distance of 105 miles. During that year negotiations were commenced for the purchase or consolidation of the King's Mountain Railroad, a line of 5 feet gauge, running between Chester and Yorkville, 22 miles, with the intention of converting it into a 3-feet gauge, to form part of the Chester and Lenoir Railroad. The negotiations were consummated April 3d, 1874, and the change of gauge and disposal of the broad gauge rolling stock commenced forthwith. On August 31st the line was opened, and the first train on the narrow gauge ran through between Chester and Yorkville.

During 1875, 27 miles were completed, bringing the road to Dallas, N. C., and construction is still going forward.

The maximum grade is 106 feet to the mile, and proportion of grade to level in entire line is 33%.

The sharpest curvature is 6° (955 feet radius), and the proportion of curvature to tangent in entire line as 1 to 2.

The weight of rail is 30 pounds to the yard.

Weight of engine 10 tons.

Average cost of road per mile, including equipment, $7,000.

Equipment, 2 locomotives, 2 passenger cars, 19 freight cars.

Operations for year ending April, 1875. Gross earnings $19,159.48. Expenses $10,412.29 (54 per cent.). Net earnings, $8,747.19.

Financial statement.—Capital stock authorized, $2,000,000. Paid in $275,000.

A. H. Davega, President, Chester, S. C.

E. Thomas, Superintendent, Chester, S. C.

F. Gardner, Chief Engineer, Chester, S. C.

CHICAGO, MILLINGTON & WESTERN RAILROAD.

This narrow gauge road was incorporated by the State of Illinois, Dec. 5th, 1872, to construct a line from Chicago to the Mississippi River at Muscatine, a distance of 200 miles. Construction was delayed till the end of 1875, when 12 miles were completed, and one hundred miles are now under contract.

The weight of rail is 30 pounds to the yard.

Financial statement.—First mortgage 7% bonds, due July 1st, 1905, $1,500,000.

Lewis Steward, President, Chicago, Ills.

J. W. Eddy, Vice President, Chicago, Ills.

Geo. N. Jackson, Secretary, Chicago, Ills.

COLORADO CENTRAL RAILROAD.

This company was organized in 1871, under the auspices of the Union Pacific Railway, to build narrow gauge lines from Golden to Central City and Georgetown, a total distance of 49 miles. At Golden connection is made with the Colorado Central standard gauge railway, which runs to Denver.

During 1872 twenty-one miles were operated, and the following year four miles additional. No mileage was completed in 1874. The total line operated on December 31st was 25 miles. Twenty four miles are under construction.

The maximum grade is 275 feet to the mile, and the average grade heavy,

The sharpest curvature 42° (136 feet radius).

The weight of rail is 32 pounds to the yard.

The weight of engines from 11 to 18 tons each, nearly all being placed over the drivers.

Equipment—6 locomotives, 3 passenger cars, 54 freight cars of all classes.

H. M. Teller, President, Central City, Col.

J. L. Overton, Superintendent, Central City, Col.

CROWN POINT RAILROAD.

This Company was organized in 1874 to build a narrow gauge railway from Crown Point, on Lake Champlain, where the furnaces of the Crown Point Iron Company are situated westward thirteen miles to their ore beds. The road was completed and put in operation during the summer of the same year.

The maximum grade is 160 feet to the mile, maintained for 10 miles, and the proportion of grade to level in entire line about 1 in 4.

The sharpest curvature is 17° (338 feet radius), and proportion of curvature to tangent in entire line as 1 to 2.

No. of trestles 13. Aggregate length 6,220 feet.

The weight of rail is 45 pounds to the yard.

Weight of engines 16 tons. 13 tons on drivers.

Average cost of road per mile, including equipment. $26,-000.

Equipment—3 locomotives, 1 passenger car, 112 freight cars.

Operations and financial statement not published.

Gen'l. John Hammond, President, Crown Point, N. Y.

A. L. Hinman, Treasurer, Crown Point, N. Y.

J. D. Hardy, Superintendent, Crown Point, N. Y.

DENVER AND RIO GRANDE RAILWAY.

This company was incorporated October 27, 1870, under the General Railroad Law of Colorado, to construct a railroad from Denver to El Paso, on the border of Mexico, and thence if suitable concessions could be obtained from the Government of Mexico, to the capital of that republic, a projected distance of about 1720 miles, of which 850 would be in the United States.

General Palmer, the President of the railway, who is well acquainted with the topography of the Rocky Mountain region, and with the proposed line of route and resources of the country, after studying the narrow gauge lines in Europe, proposed to build the Denver and Rio Grande Railway on a 2 feet 6 inch gauge. After, however, carefully weighing all the statistics and considering the interests and requirements of the section of territory through which the line would pass, it was finally decided to adopt a gauge of three feet as the one best adapted to the many and diversified wants of Southern Colorado and New Mexico. Work was commenced early in 1871, and the first spike on a narrow gauge track was driven on Friday, July 28th. The first narrow gauge train was run over the three miles of track completed, on August 16th, and the first division of 76 miles, from Denver to Colorado Springs, was opened for general traffic on October 27th, 1871. The second division, from Colorado Springs to South Pueblo, 43 miles, was completed and opened, June 15th, 1872.

On the Arkansas Valley Branch, 38 miles, from South Pueblo to the coal mines of Fremont county, were completed and put in operation November 1st, 1872, and 9 miles from coal mines to Cañon City, were constructed and opened for general traffic, July 6th, 1874. At the end of 1875 construction commenced on the extension to Trinidad, which at this date is approaching completion.

The maximum grade is 75 feet to the mile, and the average grade 36 feet to the mile.

The sharpest curvature is 19° (302.94 feet radius), and the proportion of curvature to tangent as 3 is to 5.

The weight of rail is 30 and 35 pounds to the yard.

The weight of passenger engines 12 tons.

The weight of freight engines 17 tons.

Average cost of road per mile, including equipment of 220 miles of main line, in stock and bonds, $45,000.

Equipment—13 locomotives, 12 passenger cars, 4 baggage, mail and express cars, and 323 freight cars of all classes. Miller platforms and Westinghouse brakes are in use on all the passenger trains.

Operations for year ending December 31st, 1875:—Gross earnings from 120 miles of main line, represented by $2,410,000 bonds, $360,700.—Operating expenses—$211,882 (58.74 per cent).   Net earnings—$148,818.

Financial statement—Capital stock authorized, $4,950,000; paid in, $4,950.000; funded debt, first mortgages bonds authorized, $4,950,000; sold $3,283.500; interest 7 per cent.; gold due, $1900.

Gen. Wm. I. Palmer, President, Colorado Springs, Col.
Wm. S. Jackson, Vice-President,   "   "   "
W. W. Borst, Superintendent,   "   "   "

DENVER, SOUTH PARK AND PACIFIC RAILROAD.

This company was organized in 1872 to build a narrow gauge railway from Denver, Colorado, southwesterly into the South Park, a fine agricultural, dairying and stock raising region, a projected distance of about 100 miles.   Various causes prevented the commencement of construction until 1874, when 16 miles were completed and opened to Morrison, where there are Sulphur Springs and other attractions.   During 1875 the line was extended a short distance.

The maximum grade is 105 feet to the mile.

The sharpest curvature, 20° (288 feet radius).

The weight of rail is 30 pounds to the yard.

The weight of engines 14 and 18 tons—12 and 15 tons respectively being placed over the drivers.

The operating expenses for the first six months were three-fourths of gross earnings, and the Superintendent writes that had it been broad gauge it could not have been operated with total earnings.   He considers it a success in every respect.

Hon. John Evans, President, Denver, Colorado.

Benjamin M. Gilman, Superintendent, Denver.

DES MOINES AND MINNESOTA RAILROAD.

This company was incorporated by the Legislature of Minnesota in 1873, to build a railway from Des Moines to Ames, a station on the Chicago and North-western Railway, a distance of thirty-seven miles; the line has since been extended to McGregor in Clayton county, one hundred and sixty miles further.   At first it was proposed to construct it of the standard gauge, but subsequent consideration induced the laying down of a three feet gauge track.   Grading was completed in November, 1873, and track-laying commenced at Des Moines January 12th, 1874, the line being completed and opened for traffic to Ames, July 29th.

The maximum grade is 80 feet to the mile.

The sharpest curvature 12° (478 feet radius).

The weight of rail is 30 pounds to the yard.

The weight of engines 15 tons, 12 tons being placed over the drivers.

Cost of road per mile, including equipment, $7,000.

Equipment—2 locomotives, 2 passenger cars, 2 baggage and express, 44 freight cars of all classes.

Financial Statement—Capital stock authorized, $300,000; paid in, $300,000; Funded debt: First mortgage, $130,000; Second mortgage, $70,000.   Total funded debt, $200,000; Floating debt, $20,000.

James Callanan, President, Des Moines, Iowa.

J. J. Smart, Vice President and Supt., Des Moines, Iowa.

Chas. H. Getchell, Treasurer, Des Moines, Iowa.

J. B. Stewart, Secretary, Des Moines, Iowa.

EAST BROAD TOP RAILROAD.

This company was incorporated May 24th, 1871, under the general railroad law of Pennsylvania, to construct a railway from Mount Union, on the Pennsylvania Railroad, to Robertsdale, Huntingdon county, where are situated some coal mines, a distance of 30 miles. The line was placed under construction during 1872, and the following year 11 miles were operated between Mount Union and Orbisonia, at which place are the iron furnaces of the Rock Hill Coal & Iron Co. During 1874, the nineteen miles between Orbisonia and Robertsdale were constructed, and the entire line formally opened for traffic on October 16th. The grade is very heavy and the alignment tortuous, two tunnels of 830 feet and 1,150 feet, respectively, having to be driven to reduce the grade and reach the desired point.

The maximum grade is 140 feet to the mile, and is continuous for three miles, the average grade for the entire line being 80 feet.

The sharpest curvature is 17° (338 feet radius).

The weight of rail laid is 40, 45 and 50 pounds to the yard, and the track is well ballasted, so that trains run very smoothly.

The weight of passenger engines is 17 tons.

The weight of freight engines is 25 tons.

Equipment—6 locomotives, 2 passenger cars, 2 baggage, mail and express, 176 freight cars of all classes.

The amount expended on construction up to November 30th, 1875, was $1,009,702.08.

Operations for year ending November 30th, 1875, the first year of operating:—gross earnings, $69,623.74; operating expenses, $42,864.84, (61.56 per cent.); net earnings, $26,758.90.

Financial statement—capital stock authorized, $1,000.000; paid in, $505,760; funded debt, first mortgage, 7 per cent., bonds due 1903, $500,000; floating debt, $43,044.94.

W. A. Ingham, President, 320 Walnut St., Philadelphia.

W. B. Jacobs, Secy. and Treas, 320 Walnut St., Philadelphia.

A. W. Sims, Superintendent, Orbisonia, Huntingdon Co., Pa.

EUREKA AND PALISADE RAILROAD.

This company was organized in 1873 to construct a narrow gauge railway from Eureka, Nevada, southward to Palisade, a station on the Central Pacific Railway, a distance of 90 miles. Work was commenced in 1874, and during the year 50 miles were constructed and opened to traffic about the end of the year, and in 1875 the road was completed.

The line is laid with steel rails, 40 pounds to the yard.

Estimated cost of road per mile, including equipment, $10,000.

Equipment—4 locomotives, 3 passenger cars, 58 freight cars.

Edgar Mills, President, Sacramento, Cal.

George H. Rice, Superintendent, Salt Lake City, Utah.

Woodruff & Anna, Agents, Palisade, Nev.

FARMERS' UNION RAILROAD.

This Company was incorporated by the State of Iowa, March 20th, 1875, to build a narrow gauge road from a point on the Mississippi River to Monona on the Missouri, a distance of 300 miles. About the end of the year 12 miles were placed in operation between Liscomb and Beaman, and track-laying is still going forward.

The maximum grade on division built is 53 feet to the mile, maintained for about a mile.

The sharpest curvature is 4° (1,432 feet radius).

The rail is of hard maple wood, 3½" x 6," notched into cross-ties and keyed, and estimated to last four years.

Average cost of road per mile, including equipment, $5,000.

Equipment—1 locomotive, 10 freight cars.

Financial Statement—Capital stock authorized, $2,000,000; paid in, $2,000 per mile; funded debt, first mortgage 10% bonds, $3,000 per mile.

J. W. Tripp, President, Liscomb, Iowa.

F. A. Soule, General Superintendent, Liscomb, Iowa.

GALENA AND SOUTHERN WISCONSIN RAILROAD.

This company was organized in 1871 to construct a railroad from Galena, on the Illinois Central Railroad, via Platteville to Muscoda, on the Wisconsin River, a distance of 72 miles.

During 1872–3 thirty miles were graded and bridged, and one tunnel of over 400 feet in length driven. Various causes prevented track laying until September, 1874, when the above mileage was ironed.

The maximum grade is 74 feet to the mile.

The sharpest curvature, 10° 40′ (537 feet radius).

The weight of rail is 35 pounds to the yard.

The weight of engines, 14 and 16 tons.

Cost per mile, including equipment, $11,000.

Equipment—2 locomotives, 1 baggage and smoking car, 34 freight cars of all classes.

Operations—Not reported.

Financial statement—No returns.

Darius Hawkins, President, Galena, Ills.

John Lorain, Secretary, Galena, Ills.

GOLDEN CITY AND SOUTH PLATTE RAILROAD.

This company was organized in 1871, under the laws of Colorado, to construct a narrow guage road from Golden, where connection is made with the Colorado Central Railway, south-eastward, to Acequia, a station on the Denver and Rio Grande Railway, a distance of 20 miles. During 1873 the line was graded, and the following year 18 miles were ironed, but owing to the panic, the rolling stock has not yet been obtained.

The maximum grade is 132 feet to the mile, maintained for 900 feet, and the proportion of grade to level in entire line is five-sevenths.

The sharpest curvature is 18° (319 feet radius).

The weight of rail is 30 pounds to the yard.

Estimated average cost of road per mile, including equipment, $9,750.

Financial statement—Capital stock authorized, $400,000; paid in, $126,000.

Charles C. Welch, President, Golden, Col.

E. L. Berthoud, Secretary, Golden, Col.

GRAFTON RAILROAD.

This company was organized under the general railroad law of Massachusetts in 1874, to construct a narrow gauge railway from Grafton Station, on the Boston & Albany Railroad, to Grafton Centre, a distance of three and one-tenth miles, which were constructed the same year.

The maximum grade is 105 feet to the mile.

The sharpest curvature 23° 24' (246 feet radius.)

The weight of rail is 35 pounds to the yard.

Weight of dummy engine, 6 tons.

Average cost of construction per mile, including equipment, $10,274.54.

Operations—Gross earnings, $5,965.60; operating expenses, $5,316.96; net earnings, $648.64.

Jonathan Wheeler, President, Grafton, Mass.

J. H. Wood, Superintendent, Grafton, Mass.

GREENLICK RAILROAD.

This company was incorporated by the State of Pennsylvania, October 19th, 1874, to build a narrow gauge railway from Scotdale to Chestnut Ridge, a distance of 6½ miles. During 1875, 3½ miles were completed, between Mt. Pleasant and Bradford Railroad, and Mt. Vernon mines.

The maximum grade is 135 feet to the mile, maintained for 1½ miles, and the proportion of grade to level in entire line ⅞.

The sharpest curvature is 16° (359 feet radius).

No. of bridges, 7; aggregate length, 250 feet.

No. of trestles, 2; aggregate length, 500 feet.

The weight of rail is 24 pounds to the yard.

Weight of engine, 10 tons.

Average cost of road per mile, including equipment, $8,500.

Equipment—1 locomotive, 1 passenger car, 17 freight cars.

Operations—The road is reported as doing a paying business.

Financial statement—Capital stock authorized, $50,000; paid in, $30,000.

J. M. Knapp, President, Scotdale, Pa.

Nath. Miles, Secretary, Scotdale, Pa.

HAVANA, RANTOUL AND EASTERN RAILROAD.

This company was incorporated by the Illinois Legislature in 1873 to build a narrow gauge railway from Havana, on the Illinois River, to Alvin, on the C. D. & V. Railroad, a distance of 140 miles. Construction was delayed till end of 1875, when 40 miles were completed, and the remainder is now approaching completion.

The maximum grade is 35 feet to the mile, maintained for ¾ of a mile, and the proportion of grade to level is 1 to 1½.

The sharpest curvature is 3° (1,910 feet radius), and the proportion of curvature to tangent as 1 to 222.

The weight of rail is 30 pounds to the yard.

Weight of engines, 12 tons.

Average cost of road per mile, including equipment, $6,000.

Equipment—2 locomotives, 2 passenger cars, 2 baggage and express, 85 freight cars.

Financial statement—Capital stock authorized, $1,000,000; paid in, $200,000; funded debt, 10% first mortgage bonds, due 1885, $650,000, $11,000 sold; floating debt, $50,000.

Benj. J. Gifford, President, Rantoul, Ills.

Guy D. Penfield, Secretary, Rantoul, Ills.

HOT SPRINGS RAILROAD.

This company was incorporated by the Arkansas Legislature in 1870, to build a railroad from Malvern to Hot Springs, a distance of 25 miles, but nothing was done until 1875, when the line was put under construction and completed at the end of the year.

The maximum grade is 106 feet to the mile.

The sharpest curvature is 20° (288 feet radius).

The weight of rail is 35 pounds to the yard.

Weight of engines, 15½ tons.

Average cost of road per mile, including equipment, $15,000.

Equipment—2 locomotives, 3 passenger cars, 1 baggage and express, 22 freight cars.

Financial statement—Capital stock authorized, $250,000; paid in, $250,000.

Jos. Reynolds, President, Hot Springs, Ark.

G. D. C. Rumbaugh, Engineer, Little Rock, Ark.

IOWA EASTERN RAILROAD.

This company was incorporated in 1871 to construct a narrow gauge railway from Beulah, on the Chicago, Milwaukee & St. Paul Railway, south-west via Elkader to Des Moines, a distance of about 200 miles. Work commenced in the early part of 1872, and during the summer, 15 miles were laid. In October the line was opened for traffic, without a station, engine house, water tank, turn-table and money. The only station at the south end was a cloth tent, and that at Beulah a baggage car. Box tops were put on platform cars and 16 transformed into box cars. In the face of the greatest difficulties, the railroad was kept in operation during the winter of 1872–3, all freight at Beulah having to be transhipped by hand, the grain having to be handled in sacks. In December, 1872, 100 car loads of freight were delivered to the Chicago, Milwaukee & St. Paul Railway, which made a very liberal arrangement by which the little road obtained a fair return. During 1874 one and a half miles of wooden track were laid, and the following year 3½ miles of wooden track and one mile of iron rail.

The maximum grade is 60 feet to the mile.

The weight of rail, 30 and 35 pounds to the yard.

Weight of engines, 12 tons.

Cost of road per mile, including equipment, $12,000.

Equipment—2 locomotives, 2 passenger cars, 31 freight cars.

Operations for year ending December 31, 1875—Gross earnings, $32,510.07 ; operating expenses, $20,477.15 (63 per cent.). This amount includes complete overhauling of road and rolling stock. Net earnings, $12,032.92.

Financial statement not published.

E. H. Williams, President, McGregor, Iowa.

Frank Larrabee, Secretary, McGregor, Iowa.

H. H. Kerr, Chief Engineer and Superintendent.

KANSAS CENTRAL RAILROAD.

This company was organized on the 1st of June, 1871, with the above title, to construct a railway westward from Leavenworth to Denver, with branches from Holton to Netawaka, and Clay Centre to Salinas, a total length of main line and branches as projected of 550 miles. The country to be traversed is acknowledged to be the most fertile and promising section of Kansas; the line of road passing through the most densely populated agricultural region of the State. Construction was commenced in 1872, and during that year 56 miles were completed and put in operation between Leavenworth and Holton.

The maximum grade is 75 feet to the mile.

The sharpest curvature, 12° (478 feet radius).

The weight of rail is 30 pounds to the yard.

The weight of passenger engines, 12½ tons.

The weight of freight engines, 17½ tons.

Cost of road, with equipment, per mile, $14,820.

Equipment—3 locomotives, 2 passenger cars, 91 freight cars of all classes.

Operations and financial statement not published.

L. T. Smith, President, Leavenworth, Kansas.

Paul E. Havens, Secretary, Leavenworth, Kansas.

Wm. R. Martin, Superintendent, Leavenworth, Kansas.

MARTHA'S VINEYARD RAILROAD.

This company was organized in 1874 to construct a narrow gauge railway across the Island of Martha's Vineyard, Mass., between Oak Bluffs and Katama, a distance of 9 miles, to accommodate the summer pleasure travel. Work was commenced in the early part of the year, the line being completed and open for traffic August 24th.

The maximum grade is 52 feet to the mile.

The sharpest curvature is 9° (637 feet radius).

The weight of rail is 30 pounds to the yard.

The weight of engine, 10 tons.

Average cost of road per mile, including equipment, $9,394.90.

Equipment—1 locomotive, 3 passenger cars.

The company is doing a paying business.

E. P. Carpenter, President, Foxboro, Mass.

Joseph Pease, Treasurer, Edgartown, Mass.

Henry Ripley, Superintendent, Edgartown, Mass.

MEMPHIS BRANCH RAILROAD.

This company was organized at Rome, Georgia, in 1873, to construct a narrow gauge railway from Rome westward to Gadsden, Alabama, a distance of about 17 miles, which were graded, and five miles ironed about the end of the year.

The maximum grade is 66 feet to the mile.

The sharpest curvature, 4° 30' (1,273½ feet radius).

The weight of rail is 28 pounds to the yard.

The weight of engine, 10 tons.

Cost per mile, including equipment, $13,600.

Equipment—1 locomotive, 1 passenger car, 5 freight cars of all classes.

W. S. Cothran, President, Rome, Ga.

C. H. Stillwell, Secretary and Treasurer, Rome, Ga.

C. M. Pennington, Superintendent, Rome, Ga.

MINERAL RANGE RAILROAD.

This company was chartered by the Legislature of Michigan in 1871, for the purpose of constructing a railroad from Copper Harbor, on Lake Superior, thence following the general direction of the Mineral Range (so called), southwesterly to some point on Ontanagon river, an estimated distance of 100 miles. Construction on the first division (Hancock to Calumet), 12½ miles, was commenced on the opening of the summer of 1872, and after the long winter succeeding, was resumed and carried on with all the energy requisite to overcome the obstacles presented by the hard climate and rough face of the country. Track laying was commenced August 8, 1873, and on September 8, trains were run from Hancock to Highway Crossing, 8 miles, and on October the 11th, to Calumet, 12½ miles. There has been no furthur construction.

The maximum grade is 211 feet to the mile. There is also a grade of 146 feet per mile sustained for two miles.

The sharpest curvature is 14° (410 feet radius), and the proportion of curvature to tangent in entire line is 1 to 3.23.

The weight of rail is 35 pounds to the yard.

The weight of engines, six drivers connected, 17½ and 20

tons; with the exception of two tons, all placed over the drivers.

Average cost of road per mile, including equipment, $29,-324.33.

Equipment—3 locomotives, 4 passenger cars, 24 freight cars of all classes.

Operations for year ending December 31, 1875—Gross earnings, $86,000.59; operating expenses, $55,664.41, (64.72 per cent.), net earnings, $30,336.18, out of which was paid, for interest and taxes, $24, 164.17, leaving surplus of $6,-172.01.

Financial statement—Capital stock authorized, $400,000; paid in, $112,160; funded debt, first mortgage 8 per cent. bonds, due 1888, $183,000; floating debt, $90,578.29.

Chas. E. Holland, President and Superintendent, Hancock, Michigan.

A. H. Viele, Secretary and Treasurer, Hancock, Michigan.

MONTEREY AND SALINAS VALLEY RAILROAD.

This company was organized early in 1874, by the farmers of Salinas Valley, California, who were at the mercy of railroad corporatious in that State, for the purpose of carrying their grain, etc., to the sea, instead of to San Francisco, and which would make them independent of monopoly in any form whatever. With an enterprise that does them much credit, they went to work and located a line between Salinas and Monterey, where there is deep water, a distance of 19 miles, and also erected two large warehouses, opening the line for traffic in October. It is intended to extend the railroad up the valley to Soledad, 35 miles.

The maximum grade is 100 feet to the mile.

The sharpest curvature, 10° (573 feet radius).

The weight of rail is 35 pounds to the yard.

The weight of engines, 18 tons.

Cost of road per mile, including equipment and erection of two warehouses, $13,000.

The line is reported as doing a very good business.

Financial statement not returned.

C. S. Abbott, President, Salinas City, Monterey County, California.

John Markley, Secretary, Salinas City, Monterey County, California.

MONTROSE RAILROAD-

This company was incorporated April 15, 1869, under the general law of Pennsylvania, to build a railroad between Montrose and Tunkhannock. No action was taken until April 27, 1871, when the first meeting was held and the board of directors elected. It was then resolved that the road should be built on a narrow gauge of three feet, as it would be sufficient for all the business likely to be offered, and could be constructed for so much less than a 4 feet 8½ inch gauge.

Surveys were commenced May 15th, 1871, and a favorable line, 28 miles long, located as follows: From the depot of the Pennsylvania and New York Canal and Railroad Company at Tunkhannock to Marcy's Pond, thence along the west bank of the Pond to a summit between the waters of Marcy's Pond and the Meshoppen Creek; crossing the same, it runs in a nearly direct line to the village of Springville, thence by the village of Dimock into the borough of Montrose. Grading was commenced in the summer, the Lehigh Valley Railroad Company agreeing to furnish the rails, ties, spikes and splices necessary for the superstructure as soon as it was completed. During 1872, the line was placed in running order to Springville, 14 miles, and by the end of 1873, to Allenville, 25 miles.

The maximum grade is 95 feet to the mile; the average ascending grade between Tunkhannock and Montrose being 38 feet to the mile.

The sharpest curvature is 18° (320 feet radius).

The weight of rail is 40 pounds to the yard.

The weight of engine, 15 tons.

Cost of road, including equipment, per mile, $12,844.

Equipment—2 locomotives, 2 passenger cars, 1 baggage, mail and express car, 13 freight cars of all classes.

Operations for 11 months ending Nov. 30, 1875. Gross Earnings $22,449.54. Operating Expenses, $14,292.18, (63.66 per cent.) Net Earnings, $8,157.36.

Financial statement, December 31, 1873—Capital stock authorized, $500,000; subscribed, $278,450; paid in, $248,351; funded debt, 7 per cent. bonds maturing 1892, $30,900; floating debt, $43,821.84; total liabilities, $323,072.84.

James J. Blakslee, President, Mauch Chunk, Pa.

Charles L. Brown, Secretary, Montrose, Pa.

NATCHEZ, JACKSON AND COLUMBUS RAILROAD.

This company was incorporated by the Legislature of Mississippi, in 1871, to construct a railway from Natchez, via Jackson to Columbus, a distance of about 180 miles. Work was commenced in the latter part of 1872, a gauge of 3' 6" being adopted, and the road located from Natchez northeast $25\frac{3}{4}$ miles to Fayette, the county seat of Jefferson county— the road bed being completed for 12 miles out of Natchez. The rails were laid on ten miles during 1873. On February 10, 1874, the President of the Company invited proposals for the construction, completion and equipment of the road to Fayette, the company paying no money on the contract, but offering its property and resources for the ultimate satisfaction of the contractor, which consists of bonds of the county of Adams, amounting to $134,900, bearing an interest of seven per cent., payable annually; of timber sufficient for all bridges as far as $3\frac{44}{100}$ miles from the terminus of the completed section, of one hundred tons of rails not yet laid, and the power of the company for leasing or mortgaging the road, which is now unincumbered.

Every effort to obtain late information has been unsuccessful.

W. D. Martin, President, Natchez, Miss.

J. H. Fitzpatrick, Secretary, Natchez, Miss.

S. M. Preston, Chief Engineer, Natchez, Miss.

NEVADA COUNTY RAILROAD.

This company was organized in 1874 to build a narrow gauge road from Colfax to Grass Valley, 16 miles; but nothing was done till 1875 when it was resolved to pass through Grass Valley to Nevada City, a distance of 22 miles. During 1875 fourteen miles were completed, and the entire line is now being operated.

The maximum grade is 116½ feet to the mile.

The sharpest curvature is 19° (303 feet radius).

The weight of rail is 35 pounds to the yard.

Weight of engines, 20 tons.

Equipment—2 locomotives, 2 passenger cars, 2 baggage and express, 30 freight cars.

Financial statement not published.

John C. Coleman, President, Nevada City, Col.

John F. Kidder, Superintendent, Nevada City, Col.

NORTH PACIFIC COAST RAILROAD.

This company was incorporated and certificate filed in the office of the Secretary of State of California, December 19, 1871.

The line of route is as follows: Starting at deep water at Sancelito, just opposite the City of San Francisco, with which it connects by ferries, it skirts for two miles the shore of Richardson's Bay; thence crossing an arm of the same bay by means of a substantial bridge 4,000 feet in length, it passes through Marin county, via the town of San Rafael, to Tomales, at the head of the bay of that name; thence through Sonoma county to the Russian River, crossing which four miles from its mouth, it follows near the coast of the ocean to the mouth of the Walhalla River, a distance of 115 miles, and is projected from there to Humboldt Bay, making total length of line 225 miles. The line passes through a very fertile and wealthy region. The topography of the country it traverses warranted the largest estimate of economy in first cost, equipment and operation. The narrow gauge possessing these features, it was accordingly adopted.

The surveys were made in 1872, work being commenced at various points on the main line in February of the following year. Owing to the several tunnels, bridging and trestle work, track-laying was delayed until 1874, when 51 miles were ironed and opened for traffic about the end of the year. Nine miles additional were completed in 1875, and several miles are under construction, and will shortly be put in operation.

The maximum grade is 121 feet to the mile, maintained for 2½ miles. There is also one of 85 feet, 1½ miles long, and another of 80 feet, 2 miles in length, and the average grade is exceptionally heavy.

The sharpest curvature is 22° 23′ (256 feet radius), set out on the maximum grade. The prevailing curvature is 10° to 16°; the proportion of curvature to tangent being about as 5 is to 3.

Number of lineal feet, trestle and pile bridges, 17,600.

Number of lineal feet, truss bridges, 570.

There are several tunnels on the line, one being 1250 feet in length.

The weight of rail is 35 pounds to the yard.

The weight of engines, four wheels and six wheels connected, is 22½ tons, 16 and 17 tons being placed over the drivers. One engine, on the Fairlie principle, single boiler, six wheels connected, weighs 32 tons, 24 tons being placed over the drivers.

The average cost per mile, including equipment for first division, is estimated at $23,400.

Equipment—9 locomotives, 9 passenger cars, 3 baggage mail and express, 190 freight cars of all classes.

Operations—The line being under construction, no returns have been received.

A. D. Moore, Prest., 426 California street, San Francisco, California.

Howard Schuyler, Chief Engineer, San Francisco, Cal.

Geo. F. Hartwell, Superintendent, San Francisco, Cal.

NORTH AND SOUTH OF GEORGIA RAILROAD.

This company was organized in the city of Rome, Ga., on August 11th, 1871, under and by an act of the Legislature of the State of Georgia, approved October 24, 1870, to construct a narrow gauge railway from Columbus to Rome, a distance of 130 miles, via La Grange and Carrollton.

During 1872, some 60 miles were graded, and in the latter part of the year a few miles were ironed. In 1873, 23 miles were opened for traffic between Columbus and Hamilton. Nothing further has been done, owing to the late panic, and the railway has now passed into the hands of a Receiver since its failure to pay the interest on the bonds issued it by the State.

The maximum grade is 90 feet to the mile.

The sharpest curvature 6° (955 feet radius).

The weight of rail is 30 pounds to the yard.

The weight of engines, 15 tons.

Cost per mile, including equipment, $15,000.

Equipment—2 locomotives, 2 passenger cars, 4 baggage and express, 16 freight cars of all classes.

Operations and financial statement not published.

T. E. Blanchard, President, Columbus, Ga.

Dr. Llewellen, Receiver, Columbus, Ga.

OHIO AND TOLEDO RAILROAD.

This Company was incorporated in 1872, and is a continuation of the Painesville and Youngstown Railroad, with which it connects at the latter point, running by the valley of Mill Creek to Columbiana, thence by way of Leetonia, Guilford, Hanover, Lynchburg, East Rochester, Minerva, Oneida and Carrollton, to the Conotton Valley, terminating at Cannonsburg, in the vast coal fields of Carroll and Tuscarawas counties, a total distance of 65 miles, and from thence is projected to Toledo. Work was commenced in the summer of 1874, and 22 miles, between Oneida and Guilford, built on the towing path of the old Sandy and Beaver Canal, were completed and opened for traffic in September. The balance of the road is now under construction and will shortly be in operation.

The grades and curves are very easy.

The weight of rail is 32 pounds to the yard.

The weight of engines, 16 tons.

Cost per mile, including equipment, estimated at $9,000.

Equipment—3 locomotives, 4 passenger cars, 16 freight cars of all classes.

E. R. Eckley, President, Carrollton, Ohio.

Geo. P. Davis, Treasurer, Minerva, Ohio.

S. Weaver, Secretary, Minerva, Ohio.

OLYMPIA RAILROAD.

This company was organized in 1873, at San Francisco, to construct a narrow gauge railway from Olympia, the capital of Washington Territory, to Tenino, twenty-five miles below Puget Sound, where are situated some coal lands—a distance of about 20 miles. Work was commenced in 1874, and about the end of the year the line was completed. No statistical information could be obtained.

Average cost of road per mile, including equipment, $15,000.

Financial statement—Capital stock authorized, $1,000,000.

Olympia Railroad and Mining Company, San Francisco, California.

PAINESVILLE AND YOUNGSTOWN RAILROAD.

This company was organized, and certificate of incorporation filed in the office of the Secretary of State for Ohio, November 17, 1870 ; being, we believe, the second narrow gauge railway company formed in the United States. The line of route is from Fairport Harbor on Lake Erie, via. Painesville, and the counties of Lake, Geauga, Trumbull and Mahoning to Youngstown, a distance of $64\frac{4}{10}$ miles.

The engineers commenced surveying the line on July 24th, 1871. In locating the line the advantages offered by the partially constructed road-bed of the Painesville and Hudson Railroad were availed of to Chardon, a distance of 12 miles. The company for the use of this road-bed paid $60,000.

On July 4th, 1872, twelve miles were completed and put in operation, and in the following year eleven miles additional, making the total line operated during 1873, 23 miles. Forty-one miles were completed in 1874, thus making the total amount of track laid on December 31st, 1874, 64 miles, of which only fifty miles were operated, owing to want of depot facilities, and difficulties of procuring right of way through the corporation limits of the city of Youngstown.

The maximum grade, which it was found necessary to maintain for two miles, is 82 feet per mile; there is also one of 60 feet, maintained for three miles.

The sharpest curvature is 14° (410 feet radius.)

The weight of rail is 35 pounds to the yard.

The weight of passenger engines, 12 tons.

The weight of freight engines, 18 tons.

Average cost per mile, including equipment, $19,000.

Equipment—6 locomotives, 4 passenger cars, 2 baggage, mail and express cars, 73 freight cars of all classes.

Financial Statement—According to the latest returns, capital stock authorized, $2,000,000; paid in, $571,314.

Paul Wick, President, Youngstown, Ohio.

A. B. Cornell, Secretary, Youngstown, Ohio.

Mason Evans, Assistant Secretary, Youngstown, Ohio.

L. F. M'Aleer, Superintendent, Youngstown, Ohio.

PARKER AND KARNS CITY RAILROAD.

This Company was incorporated June 30th, 1873, under the General Railroad Law of Pennsylvania, to construct a narrow gauge railway from Parker Junction, on the Alleghany River, to Karns City, in Butler county, a distance of 10 miles. The line runs up the winding valley of Bear Creek, passing through Petrolia and the lower oil regions, and is projected beyond Karns City to Millerstown. The road was placed under construction in 1873, and by the end of the year four miles were in operation. On April 8th, 1874, the line between Parker Junction and Karns City was formally opened for traffic.

The maximum grade is 96 feet to the mile, and the average for the entire line is 83 feet to the mile.

The maximum curvature on the main line is 27° (212 feet radius), on side track 47° (122 feet radius).

The weight of rail is 30 pounds to the yard.

The weight of passenger locomotives, 16½ tons.

The weight of freight locomotives, 18 tons.

The cost per mile, including equipment, $26,012.88.

Equipment—4 locomotives, 5 passenger cars, 2 baggage, mail and express, 43 freight cars of all classes.

Operations for year ending December 31st, 1874:—

During the first three months only four miles were operated, and in the latter part of the year the expenses were exceptionally heavy, so that the following figures should not be taken as a test of the road :

Gross earnings $131,689.90; operating expenses, $74,997.01. (56.9 per cent.)   Net earnings, $56,692.89.

Financial Statement—Capital stock authorized, $150,000; paid in, $75,000; funded debt, first mortgage 7 per cent. gold bonds, $63,000: floating debt, $78,442.44.

Saml. D. Karns, President, Parker, Pa.

F. Parker, Vice-President, Parker, Pa.

R. M. Moore, Auditor, Parker, Pa.

W. C. Mobley, Superintendent, Parker, Pa.

PEACHBOTTOM RAILROAD.

This company was incorporated by an Act of the General Assembly of Pennsylvania, approved March 24th, 1868.   Supplements thereto were passed at the sessions of the Legislature in 1871–2, 1872–3, granting additional privileges.   During 1872 the line was located as follows : Leaving Oxford, on the Philadelphia and Baltimore Central Railroad, it pursues a westward course through Lancaster county, crossing the Susquehanna river just opposite Peachbottom, thence northwestward to York, a distance of 60 miles.   From York it is proposed to extend the line to the eastern terminus of the East Broad Top Railroad, 85 miles, thus forming a through coal route 145 miles in length, from the great coal field of Broad Top, eighty square miles in area, to the eastern markets.   Some twelve miles were graded in 1872, and during the following year track was laid on eight miles, but was not operated.   In 1874, 38 miles were completed and put in operation, and the following year 7 miles were completed, and early in 1876 the line was finished.

The maximum grade is 105 feet to the mile, maintained for 2½ miles.

The sharpest curvature is 19° (303 feet radius).

The weight of rail is 30 pounds to the yard.

Weight of engines, 10 to 14 tons, nearly all placed over drivers.

Average cost of road per mile, including equipment, $11,500.

Equipment, 4 locomotives, 4 passenger cars, 2 baggage and express, 24 freight cars.

Financial statement: Capital stock authorized, $1,000,000, paid in, $218,552. Funded debt, first mortgage 7 per cent. bonds due 1904—total issue $650,000. Amount sold, $350,400. Floating debt, $9,264.

S. G. Boyd, President, York, Pa.

Samuel Dickey, Vice President, Oxford, Pa.

PEEKSKILL VALLEY RAILROAD.

This railway was built by the Peekskill Iron Company in 1873, from their furnaces, at Peekskill, Westchester county, to a point on the Hudson River Railroad, a distance of seven miles. The gauge of this railway is two feet, and it is the narrowest freight carrier on this continent. The superstructure and equipment is very light. The only statistical data obtained is that the weight of the engine is four tons.

Communications should be addressed to the company.

PITTSBURG AND CASTLE SHANNON RAILROAD.

This company was incorporated under the General Railroad Law of Pennsylvania, April 4th, 1868, to construct a railway from Pittsburg to Finleyville via Castle Shannon, where are situated the coal mines of the company; the line has since been projected to Waynesburg, in Greene county, 45 miles south of Pittsburg. Part of the road was purchased from the Pittsburg Coal Company, who had laid down a track of 3 feet 4 inches, which gauge has been adhered to. During 1872 three miles were placed in operation, and the following year three additional, bringing the line to Castle Shannon. In 1874 four miles were constructed, making total length of track laid, December 31st, 10 miles. The entire road is built very substantially in order to sustain a heavy coal traffic.

The maximum grade is 80 feet to the mile.

The sharpest curvature 45° 50′ (125 feet radius).

The weight of rail is 45 pounds and 60 pounds to the yard.

The weight of passenger engine, 12 tons.

The weight of freight engines, from 9 to 20 tons.

Cost per mile, including equipment, $40,000.

Equipment—6 locomotives, 7 passenger cars, 416 coal cars.

Operations for year ending December 31st, 1874: Gross earnings, $352,000; operating expenses, $280,000 (79.54 per cent.); net earnings, 72,000.

Financial Statement—Capital stock authorized, $1,000,000; paid up, $525,622.30; funded debt, first mortgage 6 per cent. bonds, $246,000; floating debt, $83,000.

M. D. Hays, President, Pittsburg, Pa.

Josiah Reamer, Secretary and Treasurer, Pittsburg, Pa.

PENNSBORO AND HARRISVILLE RAILROAD.

This company was incorporated in 1875 by the Legislature of West Virginia to build a narrow gauge railroad between the above places in Ritchie county, a distance of 9 miles. The road was first used as a horse tramway, but later in the year a small locomotive was placed on the road.

The maximum grade is 300 feet to the mile, maintained for ¾ of a mile.

The sharpest curvature is 100 feet radius.

No. of bridges, 6; aggregate length, 600 feet. No. of trestles, 1; aggregate length, 220 feet.

The weight of rail is 12 pounds to the yard, placed on wood stringers and cross ties 3 feet apart.

Weight of engine, 6½ tons with tender; 5 tons on drivers.

Average cost of road per mile, including equipment, $3,000.

Equipment—1 locomotive, 1 passenger car, 2 freight cars.

Operations—Road just opened.

Financial Statement—Capital stock authorized, $12,000; paid in, $12,000; funded debt, 1st mortgage 8% bonds, due August 6th, 1885, $15,000; floating debt, $3,000.

M. P. Kimball, President, Pennsboro, West Va.

Thos. E. Davis, Secretary and Treasurer, Pennsboro, West Va.

RIO GRANDE RAILWAY.

This Company's charter is dated August 12th, 1870, but it was not organized till May 22d, 1871, when it was resolved to build a railway from Brownsville on the Rio Grande, opposite Matamoras, Mexico, eastward to Point Isabel, in the harbor of Brazos Santiago, on the Gulf of Mexico, a distance of 22 miles, with a gauge of 3 feet 6 inches. Work was commenced in 1872, and eight miles constructed during that year. In 1873 fourteen miles were built, completing the road, when it was opened for traffic.

The maximum grade is 8 feet to the mile, and the curvature almost nil.

The weight of rail is 36 pounds to the yard.

The weight of engines is 14 tons.

The Secretary reports that they are doing a very good business.

Financial statement not published.

Antonio Longaria, Prest., Brownsville, Cameron Co., Texas.

Jos. Kleiber, Secretary, Brownsville, Cameron Co., Texas.

H. N. Zook, Superintendent, Brownsville, Cameron County, Texas.

RIPLEY RAILROAD.

This Company was organized in 1871, to build a narrow gauge road from Middletown, a station on the Memphis and Charleston Railroad, to Ripley, in Tippah county, Miss., a distance of 26 miles. Grading was commenced and completed by the Company, and the iron and equipment furnished by the Southern Security Company, who own and operate the road; the line being opened for traffic in the latter part of 1872.

The maximum grade is 106 feet to the mile.

The weight of rail is 35 pounds to the yard.

The weight of engines, 12 to 15 tons.

Cost of road, including equipment, per mile, $12,500.

Equipment—2 locomotives, 2 passenger cars, 1 baggage, 15 freight cars of all descriptions.

Operations and financial statement not published.

Communications should be addressed to the Southern Security Company, Memphis, Tenn.

SAN LUIS OBISPO AND STA. MARIA RAILROAD.

This Company was organized in 1873 to construct a narrow gauge railway from San Luis Obispo, California, to the steamer landing on the bay at Avila, thence south via Arroya Grande into Santa Maria county, a distance of about 36 miles. Work was commenced in 1874 on the division between San Luis Obispo and Avila, 9 miles, which were completed in 1875, and several miles are now under construction.

The maximum grade is 116 feet to the mile, maintained for 7,000 feet.

The sharpest curvature is 15° (383 feet radius) and the proportion of curvature to tangent in entire line 56 per cent.

No. of bridges, 6.   Aggregate length, 300 feet.

No. pieces of piling, 16.   Aggregate length 5,000 feet.

The weight of rail is 42 pounds to the yard.

Weight of engines, 16 tons.

Estimated average cost of road per mile, including equipment—$12,500.

Equipment—1 locomotive, 1 passenger car, 1 baggage and express, 10 freight cars.

Financial Statement—Capital stock, authorized $500,000.

Christopher Nelson, President, San Francisco, Cal.

W. H. Knight, Secretary, San Francisco, Cal.

L. H. Shortt, C. E. and Supt., San Luis Obispo, Cal.

SANTA CRUZ RAILROAD.

This company was organized in 1873 to build a narrow gauge railway from the harbor of Santa Cruz to Watsonville, a station on the Southern Pacific Railway, a distance of 20 miles. Grading commenced the same year, but tracklaying was delayed until the end of 1874, when 8 miles were ironed, and the following year the road was completed.

No statistical information could be obtained.

F. A. Hihn, President and Manager, Santa Cruz, California.

SUMMIT COUNTY RAILROAD.

This Company was organized in 1873 in Salt Lake City, to construct a narrow gauge railway from Echo, a station on the Union Pacific Railway, south-eastward to Coalville, a distance of about 9 miles. Work was commenced and the line completed and opened during 1873. A company has since been incorporated to build a line 35 miles in length, from Coalville westward to Salt Lake City.

The maximum grade is 300 feet to the mile.

The sharpest curvature not known.

The weight of rail is 30 pounds to the yard.

No further information obtainable.

J. A. Young, President, Salt Lake City, Utah T.

William M. Riter, Superintendent, Coalville, Summit Co., Utah T.

STOCKTON AND IONE RAILROAD.

This company was organized in 1873 to construct a narrow gauge railway from Stockton, California northwestward via Linden to Ione City in Amador county, a distance of 40 miles. Grading was commenced in 1874, but financial difficulties prevented the laying of track till 1875, when 18 miles were ironed.

The maximum grade is 53 feet to the mile.

Weight of rail, 40 pounds to the yard.

James D. Schuyler, Engineer, Stockton, Cal.

TOLEDO AND MAUMEE RAILROAD.

This company was incorporated and certificate filed in the office of the Secretary of State for Ohio, May 16th, 1873. Organization did not take place till September. The line runs between Toledo and Maumee, all in Lucas county, a distance of 8 miles, which was completed and opened for traffic August 12, 1874. The road has since been projected to Van Wert, on the Ohio State line, a distance of 80 miles, part of which is now under construction, there to connect with the 41st parallel narrow gauge railway of Indiana, which is to connect with the Keithsburg and Eastern, which will connect with the Keithsburg and Council Bluffs Railway.

On all these railways some work is being done, and when all are completed a consolidation will be effected, thus forming an air line between the great grain-growing regions of the north-west and the port of Toledo, to be known as the 41st Parallel Railroad.

The maximum grade is 25 feet to the mile, maintained for a

quarter of a mile, and the proportion of grade to level in entire line is ⅛.

The sharpest curvature is 23° 53′ (240 feet radius).

No. of trestles, one, length 150 feet.

The weight of rail is 25 pounds to the yard.

Weight of engines, 19,000 pounds, 16,500 pounds on drivers.

Average cost of road per mile, including equipment, $8,000.

Equipment—2 locomotives, 1 passenger car, 1 baggage and express, 5 freight cars.

Operations—Total gross earnings for year ending January 1, 1876, $13,563.16. Operating expenses reported as $19.48 per day, which would equal under 50%.

Financial statement—Capital stock authorized, $125,000; paid in about $50,000 ; floating debt about $15,000.

Wm. J. Wells, President, Toledo, Ohio.

Geo. W. Reynolds, Vice President, Toledo, Ohio.

TUSKEGEE RAILROAD.

This Company was organized under the laws of Alabama in 1871, to construct a narrow gauge road from Tuskegee to Chehaw, a distance of 6 miles. Work was commenced the same year, and the line completed in November.

The maximum grade is 60 feet to the mile.

The weight of rail is 25 pounds to the yard.

The weight of engine, 10 tons.

Equipment—1 locomotive, 1 passenger car, 3 freight cars of all classes.

G. W. Campbell, Superintendent, Tuskegee, Ala.

UTAH NORTHERN RAILROAD.

This Company was organized in the fall of 1871, to construct a narrow gauge railroad from Brigham, a station on the Central Pacific Railway, via Logan to Franklin, a distance of 61 miles. The line has since been extended from Brigham southward to Ogden, 25 miles, and northward to a point on the Northern Pacific Railway, in Montana, a total projected distance of 450 miles.

Work was commenced in 1872, and during that year 30

miles were constructed and operated between Brigham and Hampton.   In 1873 the line was extended 27 miles, and during 1874 the line was completed to Brigham, and from Hyde Park to Franklin, 20 miles, and the following year extended northward 10 miles—making total line in operation at the end of 1875, 87 miles.   35 miles are now under construction.

The maximum grade is 90 feet to the mile, maintained for three miles; and the proportion of grade to level in entire line is about 20 feet per mile.

The sharpest curvature is 18° (319 feet radius).

The weight of rail is 30 pounds to the yard.

Weight of engines, 13 and 18 tons; 2½ tons placed over each driver.

Average cost of road per mile, including equipment, $9,500.

Equipment—5 locomotives, 4 passenger cars, 42 freight cars of all classes.

Operations for year ending Dec. 31, 1875 : Gross earnings, $137,000.   Operating expenses, $77,000 (56.12 per cent.) Net earnings, $60,000.   Financial statement not published.

R. M. Bassett, President, Birmingham, Conn.

Moses Thatcher, Secretary, Logan, Utah.

Charles Nibley, G. F. and T. Agent, Logan, Utah.

UTAH WESTERN RAILROAD.

This company was organized in 1874 to purchase all rights and interests of the Salt Lake, Sevier Valley and Pioche narrow gauge railway, which had twenty miles of its line graded and bridged, etc.   The transfer was consummated in September and the line of route laid as follows :

Leaving Salt Lake City, it runs westward to the southern extremity of Great Salt Lake—20 miles; thence to Stockton, in Tooele county—45 miles; and from thence is projected to the Pacific.   Track laying was commenced in November, and by the end of the year 18 miles were completed and put in operation.   Construction is still going on, but report of track laid in 1875 is not yet to hand.

The maximum grade is 74 feet to the mile.

The curvature is almost nil—the alignment being very direct.

The weight of rail is 30 pounds to the yard.

The weight of engine, 19 tons.

Equipment—1 locomotive, 2 passenger cars, 18 freight cars of all classes.

Financial Statement—Capital stock, $920,000. Funded debt, $720,000.

John W. Young, President, Salt Lake City, U. T.

H. B. Clawson, Vice President, Salt Lake City, U. T.

John N. Pike, Secretary, Salt Lake City, U. T.

H. P. Kimball, Superintendent, Salt Lake City, U. T.

WALLA WALLA RAILROAD.

This company was organized in 1872, to construct a narrow gauge railway from Walla Walla, Washington Territory, eastward twenty miles to a point on the Oregon State line. Work commenced in 1873, and during that year ten miles were constructed; the following year ten miles additional, completing the line.

No statistical information could be obtained, although efforts were made to secure it.

D. S. Baker, President, Walla Walla, W. T.

WASATCH AND JORDAN VALLEY RAILROAD.

This company was incorporated in 1873, to construct a narrow gauge railway from Sandy, a station on the Utah Southern Railway, to Alta City, in Little Cottonwood Canon, where the "Emma" and other large mines are situated, a distance of about 20 miles. During 1873, twelve miles were completed and opened between Sandy and Fairfield, and in 1875 it was extended 8 miles to Alta.

The maximum grade is 287 feet to the mile. There is a grade of 250 feet to the mile continuous for 3 miles, and the ruling gradient is heavy.

The line is reported as doing a good business. No statistical information or statements returned.

Wm. Jennings, President, Salt Lake City.

Frank Fuller, Superintendent, Salt Lake City.

WEST END NARROW GAUGE RAILROAD.

This company is a reorganization of the St. Louis and Florissant, 16 miles in length, of which 8 miles were completed during 1875, and the remainder is now under construction.

The maximum grade is 105 feet to the mile.

The sharpest curvature is 20° (288 feet radius).

No. of bridges, 3 ; aggregate length, 1100 feet.

The weight of rail is 35 pounds to the yard.

Weight of engines, 12 and 20 tons.

Average cost of road per mile, including equipment, $12,000.

Equipment—2 locomotives, 3 passenger cars.

Operations—Line only opened a short time.

Financial Statement—Capital stock authorized, $150,000; paid in, $75,000.

Erastus Wells, President, St. Louis, Mo.

Wm. J. Lewis, Treasurer, St. Louis, Mo.

C. H. Sharman, Superintendent and Engineer, St. Louis, Mo.

WORCESTER AND SHREWSBURY RAILROAD.

This company was organized under the Massachusetts General Railroad Law of 1872, and certificate filed April 27, 1873, to construct a narrow gauge road from Washington square, in the City of Worcester, to the westerly shore of Lake Quinsigamond, near the dividing line between Worcester and Shrewsbury, a distance of about 3 miles, thence to Shrewsbury, the line being built to accommodate pleasure travel.

Work was commenced in May, and the road formally opened for public travel on July 31, 1873.

The maximum grade is 160 feet to the mile, partly on a 12° curve.

The sharpest curvature is 15° 40' (366.8 feet radius).

The weight of rail is 35 pounds to the yard.

The weight of engine, 11 tons.

Equipment—3 locomotives, 5 passenger cars.

Average cost of road per mile, including equipment, $15,000.

Operations for year 1875—Gross earnings, $9,947.32. Operating expenses, $7,739.59 (77.80 per cent.). Net earnings, $2,207.73. Greatest number of passengers carried in one day, 5,000.

Financial Statement—Capital stock authorized, $40,000; paid in, $35,000; floating debt, $13,000.

E. B. Stoddard, President, Worcester, Mass.

Joseph E. Davis, Treasurer, Worcester, Mass.

James Draper, Superintendent, Worcester, Mass.

WYANDOTTE, KANSAS CITY AND NORTHWEST-ERN RAILROAD.

This company was organized under the General Railroad Law of Missouri, on the 10th day of June, 1872, to construct a narrow gauge railway from Kansas City, Mo., east through the counties of Jackson, Lafayette, Saline, Howard, Boone, Callaway, Montgomery, Warren, St. Charles and St. Louis, to the city of St. Louis, a distance of about 240 miles.

The line of route passes through an exceedingly fine agricultural region, and contiguous to the road in Lafayette and Saline counties there are deposits of an excellent quality of bituminous coal. Surveys were commenced in April, 1873, but no construction on the first division, between Kansas City and Arrowrock (owing to the panic) was commenced until the spring of 1874. On June 15th the first spike was driven at Independence, Mo., and the first train ran through from Kansas City to Independence, 10 miles, August 3d. During 1875 the line was extended 7 miles, and construction is now going on rapidly.

The maximum grade is 76 feet to the mile.

There is no sharp curvature.

The weight of rail is 30 pounds to the yard.

The weight of engines, 15 tons.

Cost of road, including equipment, per mile, $18,500.

Equipment—2 locomotives, 4 passenger cars, 22 freight cars. of all classes.

Operations—Gross earnings have averaged $1,300 per month Operating expenses not published. Financial statement withheld.

Capital stock authorized, $2,000,000.

F. C. Eames, President, Kansas City, Mo.

A. L. Harris, Treasurer, Kansas City, Mo.

G. W. Vaughn, Superintendent and C. E., Kansas City, Mo.

CANADIAN NARROW GAUGE RAILWAYS.

FROM a report of Mr. Edmund Wragge, issued in 1871, we make the following extracts:

"The narrow gauge railways which have been already constructed in the Dominion of Canada, and which are also the first upon this continent, are the Toronto, Grey and Bruce Railway and the Toronto and Nipissing Railway. For some years prior to 1866, there had been scarcely any railway progress in Canada, and owing to the bad repute in which Canadian Railways were held as an investment in England, it seemed hopeless to wait until the country was able, of itself, to find the means to construct railways of the ordinary character and involving the ordinary cost.

"Mr. Geo. Laidlaw, of Toronto, who is the pioneer of narrow gauge railways upon the Continent of America, seeing no way of being able to raise the money necessary for an ordinary railway, advertised in the English newspapers for some account of how a cheap railway could be constructed, and, at that time, knowing nothing of narrow gauge railways, received answers, among others, from Mr. Carl Pihl, the government engineer of Norway, in which country the three feet six inch gauge is the national gauge; and from Sir Charles Fox & Sons, of London, who had already constructed a railway of three feet six inch gauge in India, and some two hundred miles of similar gauge railway in Queensland, Australia. With that perspicuity for which he is distinguished, Mr. Laidlaw at once saw that this class of road was the one for which he was seeking, and which, while it would afford all the accommodation likely to be needed for many years to come, could be constructed at a minimum cost, consistent with efficiency. He, therefore, immediately opened communications with the firm of Sir Charles Fox & Sons, and without going into the details of the various steps which have followed this movement, it may be stated they obtained, after a hard fight in the Legislature, where they had to meet in opposition all the railway authorities of the Dominion, charters for the construction of the Toronto, Grey and Bruce, and Toronto and Nipissing Railways, upon a gauge of three feet six inches.

The operations of these railways were so satisfactory, and the conditions of the country the same in the Province of New Brunswick and Prince Edward's Island, that their respective governments granted charters for the construction of railways with a three feet six inch gauge.

On December 31, 1875, the following railways in the British Possessions in North America had narrow gauge track laid:

	Miles Built, Including Sidings.	Total Projected Mileage.
Toronto, Grey and Bruce,	210	191
Toronto and Nipissing,	88	230
Lake Champlain and St. Lawrence,	10	100
New Brunswick,	100	170
Aroostook,	20	20
Riviere du Loup,	91	91
Prince Edward's Island,	200	200
	719	1002

During 1876 the New Brunswick and the Lake Champlain and St. Lawrence Railways expect to build or partially complete the remaining unconstructed portion of their lines.

In addition to the above mentioned railways, the following of 3 feet 6 inch gauge are under construction or projected:

Bangor & Calais Shore.

Great Southern of New Brunswick.

Kingston & Pembroke.

London, Huron & Bruce.

Credit Valley.

Fenelon Falls.

TORONTO, GREY AND BRUCE RAILROAD.

This Company was incorporated by special act in 1868, to build a narrow gauge railway of 3 feet 6 inch gauge from Toronto, via Orangeville and Mount Forest, to Sydenham, on Owen Sound, a distance of 122 miles, and also a branch from

Orangeville to Teeswater, 72 miles. Some months elapsed in educating the various counties and townships lying along the route of the railway, so that it was not until September, 1869, that the surveys were made. The following month construction commenced. During 1871–2 forty-nine miles were put in operation on the main line, between Toronto and Orangeville, and thirty-eight miles on the branch. The following year 144 miles were operated, and by the end of 1874 the entire line of 195 miles was in working order.

The alignment is of particular interest at two points on the T., G. & B. R., being marked at the crossing of the Humber River (15 miles from Toronto), and at the ascent of the Caledon Hills (35 miles from Toronto), by a series of sharp curves, combined with which are heavy grades, deep cuts and high embankments.

The maximum grade is 106 feet to the mile going north, maintained for 2¼ miles; 88 feet per mile going south, maintained for 3,000 feet, and the proportion of grade to level in entire line is 79 per cent.

The sharpest curvature is 12° 25′ (462 feet radius), and the proportion of curvature to tangent in entire line is 21.8 per cent.

The weight of rail from 35 to 58 pounds to the yard.

Weight of engines, from 16 to 42 tons.

Average cost of road per mile, including equipment, $20,000.

Equipment—20 locomotives, 12 passenger cars, 3 post-office and express, 3 smoking and baggage, 450 freight and other cars of all classes.

Operations for fiscal year ending June 30, 1875—The winter was unprecedented for its severeness, so that earnings fell off considerably from those of 1874. Gross earnings, $331,538; operating expenses, $258,104 (77.85 per cent.); net earnings, $73,434.

Financial statement—Capital stock authorized, $3,000,000; paid in, $300,000; municipal bonuses, $869,170.50; government bonuses, $231,592.00; Funded debt, $1,600,000; Floating debt, $500,000. The Company is now endeavoring to make arrangements with the Government for reduction of its floating debt.

John Gordon, President, Toronto, Canada.

Wm. Ramsay, Vice-President, Toronto, Canada.

W. Sutherland Taylor, Sec'y. and Treas., Toronto, Canada.

N. Weatherston, Genl. Supt., Toronto, Canada.

Edmund Wragge, Chief Engineer, Toronto, Canada.

TORONTO AND NIPISSING RAILROAD.

This Company was incorporated by the Canadian Legislature in March, 1868, to construct a railway of 3 feet 6 inch gauge from Toronto to Lake Nipissing, a distance of 230 miles. Work was commenced in 1869, and during the two following years some 40 miles were operated. In 1872, 64 miles, and in 1873, 88 miles between Toronto and Coboconk, the present terminus, were opened. This was the first narrow gauge railway opened for traffic on the continent of America.

The maximum grade is 106 feet to the mile.

The sharpest curvature 9° 30′ (600 feet radius).

The weight of rail is 40 and 56 pounds to the yard.

The weight of engines, from 16 to 42 tons.

Average cost of road per mile, including equipment, $15,-293.

Equipment—12 locomotives, 7 passenger cars, 3 baggage and express, 284 freight cars of all classes, 1 snow plough.

Operations for year ending June 30th, 1875—Gross earnings, $221,812.51; operating expenses, $135,733.21 (61.25 per cent); net earnings, $86,079.30.

Financial statement—Capital stock authorized, $3,000,000; paid in, $193,350; municipal bonuses, $375,072.59; government bonuses, $104,860; funded debt, $672,500, 8 per cent. bonds; floating debt, $290,801.11; total liabilities, $1,636,-573.71.

Wm. Gooderham, Jr., President, Toronto, Canada.

Alex. T. Fulton, Vice-President, Toronto, Canada.

Joseph Gray, Sec'y and Treas., Toronto, Canada.

Edmund Wragge, Chief Engineer, Toronto, Canada.

NEW BRUNSWICK RAILROAD.

This company was incorporated by the New Brunswick Government in 1870, to construct a railway of three feet six inch gauge, from Gibson, opposite Frederickton, on the St. John's River, to Edmunston on the upper St. John River, a distance of 160 miles, with a branch to Woodstock, ten miles, The road has since been projected to Riviere du Loup, a station on the Grand Trunk Railway, making a total distance of 260 miles.

Work was commenced in 1873, and 52 miles opened for traffic; the following year 48 miles were completed—the main line between Gibson and Perth and the Woodstock branch being operated during 1875. Construction is now going forward on the northern end of the main line.

The maximum grade is 85 feet to the mile.

The sharpest curvature 10°, (573 feet radius.)

The weight of rail is 45 pounds to the yard.

The weight of engines, built on the Fairlie principle, 27 tons.

The cost per mile, including equipment, will probably not exceed $13,500.

Equipment—4 locomotives, 3 passenger cars, 1 baggage and express, 40 freight cars of all classes.

Operations—Not reported.

Financial Statement—Capital stock authorized, $3,000,000; paid in, $650,000; funded debt, first mortgage 6 per cent. bonds, $1,000,000; floating debt, $43,000; total liabilities, $1,693,000.

Alex. Gibson, President, Frederickton, N. B.

J. L. Inches, Secretary and Treasurer, Frederickton, N. B.

Thos. Hoben, Superintendent, Frederickton, N. B.

PRINCE EDWARD'S ISLAND RAILROAD.

This road, of a 3 feet 6 inch gauge, which was built and is operated by the Government, traverses the whole length of the Island, from Tiguish, in the north, to Georgetown and Souris, in the east, connecting also with Summerside and Charlottetown, on the south, a total distance of main line and branches of 200 miles. Work was commenced in 1873, and fifty miles constructed during that year. In 1874 seventy miles were built, and the whole line was completed during 1875.

The maximum grade is 70 feet to the mile, and the proportion of grade to level in entire line is eighty-six per cent.

The sharpest curvature is 11° 30′ (500 feet radius), and the proportions of curvature to tangent in entire line 33½%.

No. of bridges, 46; aggregate length, 2403 feet.

The weight of rail is 40 pounds to the yard.

Weight of engines, 22 and 26 tons.

Average cost of road per mile, including equipment, $16,000.

Equipment—14 locomotives, 28 passenger cars, 168 freight cars.

Operations—Not reported.

Financial Statement—Not published.

W. McKechnie, Superintendent, Charlottetown, Prince Edward's Island.

T. Williams, Accountant, Charlottetown, Prince Edward's Island.

Observations on Narrow Gauge Railways.

BY PRACTICAL MEN.

I fully believe in this kind of road for short travel.—*President Worcester and Shrewsbury Railway.*

We are much delighted with our Narrow Gauge Road, and believe it an entire success.—*President Memphis Branch Railway.*

Have found no difficulty in working the road yet on account of gauge.—*President New Brunswick Railway.*

We are abundantly satisfied that "Narrow Gauge" (3 feet) is the only road now that will pay for the building of new railways.—*Vice-President Toledo and Maumee Railway.*

As regards our opinion of Narrow Gauge, we simply state that they cost less to construct and operate, and do as good work as the broad gauge.—*Secretary Monterey and Salinas Valley Railway.*

I consider that our experiment fully demonstrated that for safety, comfort and traffic, the Narrow Gauge is the true system. The theory grew in favor with every one connected with the Company, or who observed its working and economical construction and maintenance.—*Superintendent North and South of Georgia Railway.*

I consider Narrow Gauge Railways adapted to all localities where grades exceed 100 feet per mile, and the formation of the country necessitates curves of greater degree than 12.—*Chief Engineer Colorado Central Railway.*

So far as my experience with Narrow Gauge Railroads is concerned, I would say that I can see no reason why our road will not do as much work as any of the standard gauge local roads are now doing. Having had several years experience upon 5-feet gauge roads, I will say that for any road not having a heavy through business in connection with other standard roads, I would unhesitatingly recommend the three-feet gauge.—*Chief Engineer Galena and Southern Wisconsin Railway.*

The gauge is 3 feet 6 inches, and is all that can be wished, as far as the gauge is concerned. Our traffic is now getting so heavy that we are laying down 56-pound rails, some of iron and some of steel.—*Chief Engineer Toronto Grey and Bruce Railway.*

I consider the Narrow Gauge fully equal to all the requirements of all kinds of traffic, being cheaper to build, and cheaper and safer to operate than the standard gauge.—*President Mineral Range Railway.*

After three years' trial we are convinced that any railroad business may be done on a Narrow Gauge Road, and can be done cheaper than on the gauge now common. The construction of the Narrow Gauge Road is much cheaper than the proportion between that and the common gauge would seem to indicate. The bridges, with proportionately less material, are much stronger. Tunnels require little or no strengthening. The repair of road and machinery is trifling.—*President Pittsburg and Castle Shannon Railway.*

We have been operating this road since the fall of 1872, and the Narrow Gauge has given entire satisfaction.—*Superintendent Arkansas Central Railway.*

The experience of this Company in every instance confirms their opinion of the efficiency of the Narrow Gauge system, and they think it fully proven that a three-feet gauge is capable of doing all the business required of any ordinary road.—*Secretary Painesville and Youngstown Railway.*

I would state that our road carries the freight between these two points with quite as much facility as the former 5-feet track. The Superintendent reports that he uses only ⅓ of the amount of fuel that was formerly used.—*Chief Engineer Chester and Lenoir Railway.*

We are perfectly satisfied, from the workings of our road, that the Narrow Gauge system is the plan on which all roads of the South should have been constructed. We consider it perfectly adequate to meet every emergency in traffic; in fact, we believe it superior in point of capacity. We have been operating our road since November, 1871, and have never had an accident. We consider the Narrow Gauge system to be superior in point of security, economy and convenience.—*Superintendent Tuskegee Railway.*

We are perfectly satisfied that the three feet gauge is all that is required for the demands of commerce. We have all we can do in the way of both freights and passengers. The present looks favorable, and the cost being much less than broad gauge we are able to freight under the Iowa Tariff Laws with a fair profit.—*Vice-President Des Moines and Minnesota Railway.*

That this Company was able, notwithstanding a panic which caused the failure of 77 railroads in the United States, to meet all its obligations promptly and survive the gale, is a matter worthy of congratulation. It is to be attributed, chiefly, to the fact that the route occupied is one which possessed the elements for a good local trade, and that each division was able to follow the principle of "pay as you go;" also to the fact that the *Narrow Gauge* permitted an economy in building and operating without which we could not have avoided the common fate. With so new a line, had the additional interest upon capital and cost of operating required by the standard gauge been imposed upon us, we could hardly have escaped.—*President Denver and Rio Grande Railway.*

"Forney" locomotive for the first two-foot gauge line in America, the Billerica & Bedford Railroad. Built for cab-in-front operation by the Hinkley Locomotive Works, Boston, Massachusetts

Shay geared locomotive for the two-foot gauge Gilpin Tramway of Colorado, 1887. Built by Lima Locomotive Works, Lima, Ohio. Two cylinders, 7x7". Drivers, 24". Weight, 20,000 pounds

DIRECTORY OF NARROW GAUGE RAILWAYS 1871-1949

The compilation of a list of narrow gauge railroads of the United States was undertaken with temerity. The elusive nature of corporate identities, mergers, leases, and dissolutions of railroads, as well as the inadequacy of railroad reports made the work difficult.

To clarify the directory the following will assist the reader. Only railroads that actually operated are included. Paper roads and roads planned are not taken into consideration. As this book deals exclusively with narrow gauge railroads, research ends with the date the line was standard-gauged. In the directory the name of the railroad, termini, mileage, date built, date standard-gauged or abandoned are listed in that order. Predecessor railroads are designated by a letter in parenthesis, *i.e.,* (A). Successor roads are shown with a numeral in parenthesis, *i.e.,* (1).

The narrow gauge idea applied favorably to logging, mining and various other industrial enterprises. A cross section of these lines is included in the appended list of private roads in operation prior to 1895. This list is by no means complete because in the early 1890's private railroads were no longer listed in detail in reports and become fugitive. Inclusion of these lines is merely in way of giving the reader an insight into the elusive character of the narrow gauge. Furthermore it will serve as a nucleus for additional research.

The Denver & Rio Grande is conceded by historians to be the first narrow gauge railroad ever to operate in the United States. It may be the first 3' gauge, which is considered "standard" narrow gauge practice, but the 4' 1" Hecla & Torch Lake of Michigan, built in 1868, appears to precede the D. & R.G. by three years. Decidedly of interest to historians is the fact that the first two-foot gauge railroad built in the country was the Billerica and Bedford of Massachusetts in 1877. It blew up financially, however, in about a year and was abandoned — decidedly it should have had a better fate.

In a few cases railroads were first built standard gauge and then narrow-gauged. A good example of this is the Potomac, Fredericksburg and Piedmont which was narrow-gauged from the 4′ 8½″ Fredericksburg and Gordonville. In 1923 the Farmington Branch of the Denver & Rio Grande Western, which was built standard gauge, was narrow-gauged. Why the D. & R.G. ever built a standard gauge line south from Durango, the narrow gauge capital of the U.S., is a mystery that can only be attributed to the fact that the railroad planned to eventually standard-gauge their entire system.

One railroad, the Lancaster Reading Narrow Gauge Railroad, is not listed because, while projected as a 3′ gauge line, it was built to standard gauge, perhaps in opposition to the odd gauges that abounded at the time of its construction in 1875. The major portion of the Erie at that time was 6′ gauge while a host of other roads had everything from 4′ 8½″ up — there was even a mule-power lumber road of 8′ 9″! One of the most unnerving things found in compiling the directory was a lumber road listed as having a gauge of 56 feet! Upon further research this was found to be a typographical error and the road had a proper gauge of 56″.

The largest system of narrow gauge railroads was and still is in Colorado. While many of the lines have been abandoned, the Denver & Rio Grande still operates several hundred miles of narrow gauge track with the only daily first class narrow gauge train, the "San Juan," complete with diner-lounge, which can't quite make up its mind whether it wants to be in its home state of Colorado or New Mexico while it traverses the spectacularly tortuous Cumbres Pass en route to Durango from Alamosa.

The Toledo, Cincinnati & St. Louis boasted of 800-odd miles of track in Ohio prior to its dissolution in 1884. Ohio and Pennsylvania were the most narrow-gauged states in the East. Maine has long been known as the stamping ground of the two-footers. In the West, California and Nevada had the lion's share of narrow gauges.

In cross-checking the directory with Fleming's list, the reader will find a few roads missing. In example are the Alameda, Oakland & Piedmont and the Stockton & Ione. The former is omitted from the revised list as it was a horse-power railroad, while the latter was a line graded and partially ironed but financial difficulty overtook the enterprise before a train ever operated.

Poor's *Manuals of Railroads,* Interstate Commerce reports, the well-known *Official Guide of Railways of the United States,* annual reports of railroads, *Trains* and *Railroad* magazines, reports of various state railroad commissions, bulletins of the California-Nevada Railroad Historical Society, and the Railway & Locomotive Historical Society, periodicals, and many published and unpublished works were used in the compilation of this directory.

The shortcomings of this list are fully realized. There are many dates left blank because the histories of some railroads vanished from the printed record into seemingly thin air. The majority of railroads listed, however, are as complete as research material available made possible. Perhaps with the help of those more intimately acquainted with their "favorite narrow 'gauge railroad" the directory can be revised and made more complete in a future edition. Histories of some lines came easily — others were rather elusive, to say the least. At times the work seemed impossible to assemble. The fascination of following the history of a railroad from its inception to demise or standardization was its own reward.

The compiler wishes to acknowledge the valuable assistance of Jeannette Hitchcock of Hopkins Transportation Library; Leland Stanford, Jr., University; Elizabeth O. Cullen, librarian of the Association of American Railroads; G. F. Dodge, of the Denver & Rio Grande Western; David Myrick, H. T. Crittenden, and T. G. Wurm, devotees of the narrow gauge; Clement Fisher, Jr., of the Santa Fe; Randall V. Mills; and to my wife, Audrey, who, more than anyone else, made it possible for me to pursue the directory to its completion.

BRIAN THOMPSON

Oakland, California, 1949.

DIRECTORY OF NARROW GAUGE RAILWAYS

ALABAMA

NAME	GGE.	TERMINI	MILES	BUILT	S.G.	ABD.
ANNISTON & ATLANTIC	3'	Anniston to Sylacauga	52.36	1886	1891	
(A)Clifton	3'	Jenifer to Ironton	9			
(1)Alabama Mineral (1890)						
(2)Louisville & Nashville						
EAST & WEST OF ALABAMA	3'	Cartersville, Ga. to Pell City	117.6	1882	1891	
		Warners to Tecumseh	1.5			
(A)Cherokee	3'	Cartersville to Epsom Hill	46			
(1)East & West (1893)						
MONTGOMERY SOUTHERN RY.	3'	Montgomery to Live Oak	45	1882	1889	
(1)Montgomery & Florida Ry. (1886)						
NOTTINGHAM RR & IRON CO.	3'	Nottingham to Coosa River		1888	1890	
TOMBIGBEE & NORTHERN RY. (1900)	3'	Tombigbee River to Turners	35			1905
		Turners to Higdons	5			
		Nannahubba to Turners	33			
(A)Seaboard of Alabama				1891		
(1)Tombigbee Valley (1904)						
TUSKEGEE	3'	Tuskegee to Chehaw	5.5	1871		

ARIZONA

NAME	GGE.	TERMINI	MILES	BUILT	S.G.	ABD.
ARIZONA & NEW MEXICO	3'	Lordsburg N.M. to Clifton Ariz.	71	1883		
(A)Clifton & Southern Pacific						
(1)Southern Pacific.						
ARIZONA N.G.	3'	Tucson Northward	10	1882		1893
Tucson Globe & No. (1887)						
CORONADO OF ARIZONA	1'8+3'	Clifton to Morenci				1920
MAGMA ARIZONA	3'	Superior to Magma				
MORENCI SOUTHERN	3'	Morenci to Guthrie	18	1902		1923
(1)E.P. & S.W.						
SHANNON ARIZONA	3'	Metcalf to Clifton	10.5	1910		
UNITED VERDE & PAC. RY.	3'	Jerome to Jerome Jct.	26.3	1894		

ARKANSAS

NAME	GGE.	TERMINI	MILES	BUILT	S.G.	ABD.
ARKANSAS MIDLAND	3'	Helena to Clarendon	50	1871	1887	
		Pine City to Brinkley	24			
(A)Arkansas Central (Chg. 3',1833)	3'6"					
(A)Helena & Indian Bay						
(1)St. Louis Iron Mt. & So. (1909)						
BATESVILLE & BRINKLEY (1882)	3'	Brinkley to Jacksonport	58	1884	1890	
(A)Cotton Plant	3'6"			1879		
(1)White & Black River Valley (1890)						
CACHE VALLEY	3'	Sedgwick to Gage	19	1882	1904	
(A)Black & Cache River						
COTTON BELT & NORTHERN	3'	Onalaska to Tulip Creek	17			
		Bierne to Hartley	7			
		Onalaska to Pritchard	3.5			
		Gaughen Jct. to Proctor	6			
HOT SPRINGS BRANCH	3'	Malvern to Hot Springs	25	1875		
IRON MT. & HELENA	3'6"	Helena to Marianna	27	1880		
(1)St. Louis Iron Mt. & So. (1882)						
PINE BLUFF MONROE & NEW ORLEANS	3'	Rob Roy to English	30	1884		1934
		Rob Roy to Astor Pt.	15			
(A)Pine Bluff & Swan Lake						
(A)Texas & St. Louis Ry.						
(1)Pine Bluff & Eastern						
(2)Pine Bluff & Arkansas River (1898)						
SOUTHWEST ARKANSAS & INDIAN TERRITORY RY.	3'	Smithton to Pike City	32	1887	189-	
TEXAS & ST. LOUIS RY.	3'	Texarkana to Birds Pt. Mo.	417.8	1881	1886	
		Paw Paw Jct. to New Madrid	5.7			
		McNeil to Magnolia	6.81			

CALIFORNIA

NAME	GGE.	TERMINI	MILES	BUILT	S.G.	ABD.
ARCATA & MAD RIVER	3'9½"	Arcata to Korbel	12	1883	1942	
BODIE & BENTON	3'	Bodie to Mono Mills	32	1881		1915
		Mono to Woodyard	2.5	1882		
		Bodie to Standard Mine	1.5	1882		
(1)Bodie Ry. & Lumber Co. (1895)						
BORATE & DAGGETT	3'	Daggett to Borate	15			1908
CALIFORNIA & NEVADA	3'	Oakland to Bryants	23	1886		1903
(1)Oakland & East Side		Oakland to Richmond (1903)				
(2)A.T. & S.F. (C.A. & S.F.) (1912)						
CENTRAL CALIFORNIA	3'				1912	
CHINO VALLEY	3'6"	Ontario to Harrington Station	10	1888		1911
		Chino to Ontario	6			
		Chino to Dairy	4			
COLUSA & LAKE	3'	Colusa to Sites	22	1886		1916
DIAMOND & CALDOR	3'	Diamond Springs to Caldor	33.1	1902		
DEATH VALLEY	3'	Death Valley Jct. to Ryan	20	1909		1931
EMPIRE CITY	3'	Tuolumne Co.				
HETCH HETCHY & YOSEMITE VALLEYS RY.	3'	Tuolumne 35 miles east	35	1901		
(1)Westside Lumber Co.						
IRON MOUNTAIN	3'	Keswick to Iron Mountain	11	1896		1929
LAKE TAHOE RY. & TRANS.	3'	Truckee to Tahoe City	15	1900	1926	1943
(1)S.P. Co. (1925)						
LAKE VALLEY N.G.	3'	Bijou Southward up Lake Vy.	13	1885		1897
LOS ANGELES & GLENDALE	3'	Los Angeles to Glendale	8.5	1888	1911	
(1)Los Angeles Pasadena & Glendale Ry.						
(2)Los Angeles Interurban Ry. (1904)						
(3)Pacific Electric (1911)						
LOS ANGELES & REDONDO	3'	Los Angeles to Redondo Plus Other track	27	1890	3'6"- 1903	
(1)L.A. Ry. 24 Miles - 1910	3'6"					
(1)P.E. 21 Miles - 1910 S.G. 1910						
MENDOCINO	3'	Cuffy's Cove to Helmkes Mill	4	1876		
MONTEREY & SALINAS VY.	3'	Salinas to Monterey	18.5	1875	1881	
(1)S.P. (1881)						
NEVADA CALIF. & OREGON	3'	Reno to Camp Ham	45.5	'81-'84		
		Camp Ham to Liegan	24.5	1890		
		Liegan to Amadee	9	1890		
		Amadee to Termo	50.6	1900		
		Termo to Madeline	14.3	1902		
		Madeline to Likely	20.4	1907		
		Likely to Alturas	80	1908		
		Alturas to Lakeview	56	1912		
(A)Sierra Valley & Mohawk	3'	Plumas Jct. Kirby Mill	23	1894		
(1)Sierra Valleys Ry.		Kirby Mill to Clio	13	1895		
(2)Sierra Valley & Mohawk Ry. (1911)						
(3)N.C.O. (1915)		Clio to Davies Mill	2.67	1916		
		Hackstaff to Wendel				1922
(1)Western Pacific (1917)		Hackstaff to Reno (33M-S.G.)	64.8	(Rest aband.)-1918		
		Plumas Jct. to Davies Mill	39.4			
(2)Southern Pacific (1926)		Wendel to Alturas			1927	
		Alturas to Lakeview			1928	
NEVADA COUNTY NARROW GAUGE	3'	Colfax to Grass Valley	22.64	1876		1942
NORTHWESTERN PACIFIC						
North Pacific Coast	3'	Sausalito to Duncans Mills	74.25	1875		1933
(1)North Shore		Jct. to San Rafael	2			
San Rafael & San Quentin	3'	San Quentin to San Rafael	3.50	1871		
Northwestern	3'	Duncans Mills to Ingrams	7.5		1911	
Sonoma & Santa Rosa	3'	Sonoma to Santa Rosa	6.5	1882		
Sonoma Valley	3'	Sonoma to Sonoma Landing	15	1880		
PATTERSON & WESTERN	3'	Patterson to Jones	28	1916		1920
PAJARO VALLEY CONS.	3'	Watsonville to Spreckles	27.24	1898		1929
		Spreckles Jct. to Alisal	6.7			
		Bridge to Buena Vista	5.36	1905		
		Salinas Jct. to Salinas	2.25	1907		
SALMON CREEK	3'	Mendocino County	10	1885		
SAN BERNARDINO & REDLANDS	3'	San Bernardino to Motor Jct.	7.24	1888	1892	
(1)S.P. (1892)						

CALIFORNIA

NAME	GGE.	TERMINI	MILES	BUILT	S.G.	ABD.
SAN JOAQUIN & SIERRA						
NEVADA	3'	Bracks to Valley Spring	40.9	1885	1897	
(1)S.P.		Bracks to Woodbridge	10.6	1882		1897
SAN LUIS OBISPO & SANTA						
MARIA VALLEY	3'	Port Harford to San Luis Obispo	10.75	1876		1940
(1)Pacific Coast		San Luis Obispo to Santa Maria		1882		1940
SANTA CRUZ	3'	Santa Cruz to Pajaro Depot	21.50	1876	1882	
(1)S.P. (1882)						
S. CALIF. MOTOR ROAD	3'	San Bernardino to Riverside	12	1889	1896	
(1)Pacific Imp. Co.						
(2)S.P. Co.						
SOUTH PACIFIC COAST RY.						
BAY & COAST	3'	Alameda Jct. to San Antonio Jct.		1881	'05-6	
		Alameda Jct. to Newark		1878	'05-6	
Felton & Pescadero	3'	Felton to Boulder Creek	7.4	1885	'06-7	1934
Oakland Township	3'	Oakland Jct. to 12th Street	.7	1881	'05-6	1933
		12th Street to 14th Street	.2	1886	'05-6	1933
Santa Cruz & Felton	3'	Old Felton to Santa Cruz	7.8	1875	'06-7	
San Francisco & Colo. River	3'	Alameda Mole to Alameda Jct.	2.6	1884	'05-6	1944
South Pacific Coast	3'	Newark to Santa Clara		1877	'05-6	
		Santa Clara to Los Gatos		1878	'06-7	
		Los Gatos to Big Trees		1880	'06-7	
		Dumbarton Pt. to Newark	4.4	1876		1880
		Newark to Centerville		1882		1908
Almaden Branch	3'	Campbell to New Almaden	9.6	1886	'08-9	
Abandonments of S.P.C.		High Street to Mulford				1906
		Los Gatos to Olympia				1940
		La Franc to Almaden Jct.				1934
		Campbell to La Franc				1937
(1)S.P. 1906						
YOSEMITE SHORT LINE	3'	Jamestown to Jacksonville	20	1900		191

COLORADO

NAME	GGE.	TERMINI	MILES	BUILT	S.G.	ABD.
ARGENTINE CENTRAL	3'	Silver Plume to Summit of Mt. McClellan	16	1906		1918
(1)Geotwn. & Gray's Pk. (1912)						
(2)Argentine & Gray's Pk. (1912)						
ASPEN & WESTERN RY.	3'	Carbondale to Thompson Creek Mines	13	1888	1894	1941
(1)Crystal River (1892)						
(2)Crystal River & San Juan						
BOOK CLIFF (1899)	3'	Gr. Jct. to Little Bk. Cliff Mines	12	1890	1895	1921
(A)Colo. Wyo. & Great Northern						
(A)Little Book Cliff Ry.						
CANON CITY & CRIPPLE CREEK	3'	Canon City to Oro Junta	7	1900		1914
COLORADO CENTRAL	3'	Forks Creek to Georgetown	25	1877		
		Golden to Forks Creek	13.18	1872		
		Forks Creek to Black Hawk	7.72	1872		
		Black Hawk to Central City	4.02	1878		
(1)U.P.D. & G. (1890)						
(2)C. & S. (1898)						
COLORADO EASTERN RY.	3'	Denver to Scranton	17	1886		1916
(A)Denver Land & Coal Co.						
COLORADO NORTHERN	3'	Denver toward Longmont	11	1883		
(A)Denver Longmont & W'n.						
(1)Denver Utah & Pacific (1884)						
COLORADO NORTHWESTERN RY.	3'	Boulder to Ward	26.1	1898		1919
		Sunset to Eldora	22.6	1905		1919
		New Market Ext.	2.0			1919
(1)Denver Boulder & W. (1909)						
COLORADO & SOUTHERN						
(See Denver, South Park & Pacific Ry., etc.)						
DENVER CIRCLE	3'6"	In Denver				
(1)Denver & Santa Fe.(1887)						
DENVER LEADVILLE &						
GUNNISON RY.	3'	All roads listed under Denver South Park & Pacific Ry. plus Kokomo to Wilfleys Mill	1.14	1895		1905
(1)C. & S. (1898)						
DENVER & MIDDLE PARK	3'	Golden to Glencoe				
(A)Denver Union Pac. & Gulf						
DENVER & RIO GRANDE	3'	Denver to Pueblo	118	1872	1890	
		Pueblo to Canon Coal Mines	37	1872	1890	
		Pueblo to El Morro	86.5	1876	1890	1936
		Cuchora Jct. to La Veta	21.6	1876	1890	
		La Veta to Garland	37.4	1876	1900	

NAME	GGE.	TERMINI	MILES	BUILT	S.G.	ABD.
		Garland to Alamosa	24	1878	1900	
		Canon Coal Mines to Canon City	8	1876	1890	
		Canon City to Leadville	117.5	1880	1890	
		Leadville to Robinson	16	1880	1890	1923
		Malta towards Radcliffe.	9.8	1880	1890	
		Colorado City to Manitou	5.3	1880	1898	1939
		Antonito to Espanola, N.M.	91.2	1880		1941
		Douglas to Madge Quarry	2.6	1881	1890	1902
		Coal Mine Branches	2.3	1881		
		Canon City to Westcliffe	31.2	1881		1890
		Placer to Trinchera Mine	2.1	1881		1908
		Calumet to Hecla Iron Mine	6.85	1881		1923
		Robinson to Wheeler	8.3	1881		1923
		Chama to Durango	107.3	1881		
		Poncha to Gunnison	69.1	1881		
		Poncha to Maysville	6.9	1881		
		Mears Jct. to Hot Springs Iron Mine.	27.6 .	1881		
		Gunnison to Crested Butte	29.4	1881		
		Cranes Park to Red Cliff	21.2	1881	1890	
		Alamosa to Wagon Wheel Gap	46.2	1881	1903	
		Red Cliff to Rock Creek	2.8	1882	1890	
		Durango to Silverton	44.8	1882		
		Wheelers to Dillon	11.36	1882		1923
		Maysville to Chaffee	9.38			
		O'Brien Quarry Line	1.8	1880		1908
		Montrose to Ouray	35.78	1887		
		Villa Grove to Orient	8.02	1881		1940
		Wagon Wheel Gap to Creede	10	1801	1903	
		Lake Jct. to Lake City	36	1889		1932
		Pagosa Jct. to Pagosa Springs	31	1900		1935
		Aberdeen Jct. to Aberdeen	4.49	1889		1904
		El Moro to Engleville	6.4	1877	1888	1913
		Glenwood Springs to Rifle Creek	26.63	1888	1890	
		Rock Ck. to Glenwood Springs	63.4	188-	1890	
		Alamosa to Antonito	26.61	1880	1901	
		Montrose to Grand Jct.	72.5	1882	1906	
		Delta to Somerset	43.06	1902	1906	
		Crested Butte to Floresta				
		Crested Butte to Anthracite				
		Gunnison to Baldwin	19.36			
		Chama to Antonito	63.8	1881		
		Rifle Creek to Grand Jct.	63	1888	1890	
		Grand Jct. to State Line	30.5	1882	1890	
		Parlin to Pitkin	17.90			
		Durango to Farmington(Blt.-S.G.)	47.66	1903	N.G.-	1923.
		Taos Jct. to La Medera	16.43			1914
		Mineral Hot Springs to Alamosa	45.84	1882		
	3′	Sapinero to Cedar Creek	27.23			1949
DVR. S. PARK & HILL TOP RY. (1)Denver Leadville & Gunnison Ry. (2)C. & S. (1898)	3′	Hill Top Jct. to Leavick	11.33	1896		
DENVER S. PARK & PAC. RY.	3′	Denver to Morrison	17.39	1874		
		Sheridan Jct. to Webster	62	1879		
		Webster to McGees	57.13	1880		
		McGees to Buena Vista	8.82	1880		
		Macune to Con. D. & R. G. R.R.	1	1880		
		Nathrop to St. Elmo	14.63	1880		
		Como to King Coal Mines	3.27	1880		1899
		St. Elmo to Alpine Tunnel	10.47	1881		
		Garos to Fairplay	9.96	1881		1938
		Como to Boreas	10.60	1881		
		Alpine Tunnel to Gunnison	40.13	1882		
		Boreas to Keystone	24.60	1883		
		Fairplay to Alma	5.45	1882	{Sold D.& R.	
		Gunnison to Old Baldwin Mine	17.39	1883	G.W. 1937	
		Castleton up Ohio Creek	2.95	1883		
		Dickey to Kokomo	14.97	1883		
		Buena Vista to Conn. Old Line	1.56	1884		
		Kokomo to Leadville	19.97	1884		
		Macune to Nathrop	5.35	1884		
		Schwanders to Trout Ck. Conn.	1.09	1884		1905
	3′	Nathrop -- (New Main Line)	0.48	1885		
Abandonments	3′	Sheridan Jct. to Morrison	9.76			'34-38
		Garos to Macune	27.38			1922
		Hancock to Quartz	13.22			1923

COLORADO

Cont'd

NAME	GGE.	TERMINI	MILES	BUILT	S.G.	ABD.
		Parlin to Gunnison	11.30			1923
		Macune to Hancock & Buena V.	30.74			1926
		Quartz to Parlan	18.22			1934
		S. Platte to Climax & Branches	158.21			1938
		Chatfield to South Platte	15.50			1942
		Denver to Chatfield	8.01		1939	
		Climax to Leadville	14.05		1943	
(1)Dnvr. Leadville & Gunnison Ry. (1889)						
(2)C. & S. (1898)						
DENVER & SOUTH PLATTE	3'6"	Englewood to Littleton.	10			
DENVER UTAH & PACIFIC	3'	Denver to Lyons, Colo.	43.49	1885	1890	
		Branches to Coal Mines	5.81	1888	1890	
(A)Colorado & Northern						
(1)CB & Q.						
DENVER W. & PACIFIC RY.		Denver to D&I Jct.	15.66	1886		
FLORENCE & CRIPPLE CREEK	3'	Florence to Cripple Creek	39.53	1894		1915
(A)Golden Circle		Victor to Vista Grand	5.71	1896		
(1)Denver & S. West						
(2)Cripple Ck. Central (1904)						
GEORGETOWN BRECKENRIDGE & LEADVILLE RY.	3'	Georgetown to Graymont	8.47	1884		
(1)U.P.D.&G. (1890)						
(2)C.&.S. (1898)						
GILPIN (1906)	2'	Central City & Blackhawk	24			1917
(A)Gilpin County Tramway				1886		
GREELEY SALT L. & PAC. RY.	3'	Boulder to Sunset	14.43	1883		1894
(1)U.P.D.&G. (1890)						
LEADVILLE MINERAL BELT RY.	3'	Leadville Mineral Belt	2.34	1900		
(1)C.&S. (1900)						
MONTEZUMA LUMBER CO.	3'	Dolores				
RIO GRANDE & PAGOSA SPRINGS (SEE D.&.R.G.)						
RIO GRANDE SOUTHERN	3'	Ridgway to Durango	162.6	1892		
		Vance Jct. to Pandora	9.8			
SILVERTON	3'	Silverton to Ironton	20	1887		1926
SILVERTON GLADSTONE & NORTHERLY	3'	Silverton to Gladstone	7	1899		1925
SILVERTON NORTHERN	3'	Silverton to Animus Forks	14	1905		1942
		Havardsville to Green Mt.	2			
SOUTH PARK & LEADVILLE SHORTLINE	3'	London Jct. to London Mines	7.50	1883		
(A)London S.Park & Leadville						
UINTAH	3	Watson & Rainbow to Mack	68.5	1905		1939

FLORIDA

NAME	GGE.	TERMINI	MILES	BUILT	S.G.	ABD.
DE LAND & ST. JOHNS	3'	St. Johns River to DeLand	6	1885	1887	
(1)Jacksonville, Tampa & Key West (1889)						
(2)Fla. East Coast (1889)						
FLORIDA & GEORGIA	3'	Thaggard to Wellborn	30			1915
FLORIDA SOUTHERN RY.	3'	Palatka to Brooksville & Branches	178.75	1882	189-	
		Bartowe to Trabue	80.79			
(A)St. Johns & Lake Eustis Ry.	3'	Leesburg to Lane Park	23	1885	1896	
		Ft. Mason to Astor	25			
GREEN COVE & MIDLAND RY.	3'	Green C. Spring to Sharon	10	1883	Prior 1900	
(1)Western Ry. of Florida						
JACKSONVILLE ST. AUGUSTINE & HALIFAX RIVER	3'	S. Jacksonville to St. Augustine	37.03	1883	1895	
(1)Jacksonville St. Augustine & Indian River (1893)						
(2)Fla. East Coast (1895)						
JACKSONVILLE & ATLANTIC	3'	Jacksonville to Pablo Beach	17.3	1884	1899	
(1)Fla. East Coast (1899)						
ORANGE BELT RY.	3'	Sanford to St. Petersburg	153.04	1889	1898	
(1)Sanford & St. Petersburg Ry. (1893)						
PENINSULAR	3'	Waldo to Orange Lake	20	1884		
SANFORD & INDIAN RIVER	3'	Sanford to Lake Charm	17.32		1891	
(1) S. Florida (1891)						
(2)Savannah Fla. & W. (1893)						
(3)Atlantic Coast Line						
ST. AUGUSTINE & S. BEACH	3'	St. Augustine to South Beach	5	1889		
(1)St. Johns Lt. & Power Co. (1906)						
WESTERN RY. OF FLORIDA	3'6"	Sharon to Belmore	5.5	1887	Prior 1900	
(1)Southwestern (1892)						

GEORGIA

NAME	GGE.	TERMINI	MILES	BUILT	S.G.	ABD.
AMERICUS PRESTON & LUMPKIN	3'	Louvale to Abbeville	112	1887	1891	
(1)Savanah Americus & Montgomery						
AUGUSTA GIBSON & SANDERSVILLE	3'	Augusta to Sandersville	80	1886	1895	
(1)Augusta So. (1893)						
(2)Southern (1897)						
BOWDEN LITHIA SPRINGS	3'	Lithia Springs to Anstell	2.5	1885		
(1)Bowden Lithia Springs Short Line (1895)						
CHEROKEE	3'&5'	Cartersville to Essom Hill	46	1871	1890	
(1)E.&W. of Alabama (1886)						
(2)Seabord Air Line						
COLUMBUS & ROME RY.	3'	Columbus to Greenville	50	1885	1895	
(A)N.&S. Ry. (1877 - 1880)						
(1)Savanah & Western (1888)						
(2)Central of Georgia						
ELBERTON AIR LINE	3'	Elberton to Tocoa City	50	1878	1891	
(1)Richmond & Danville						
(2)Southern						
GAINESVILLE & DAHLONEGA	3'	Gainesville to Dahlonega	26	1878		1895
GAINESVILLE JEFFERSON & SO.	3'	Gainesville to Social Circle	52	1884		
		Florence to Jefferson	13			
(A)Walton						
(1)Georgia						
GAINESVILLE MIDLAND RY. Combo.	3'	Belmont to Monroe	32			
GREENVILLE COLUMBUS & BIRMINGHAM	3'			1882		
(See Mississippi)						
(1)Georgia Pacific						
HARTWELL	3'	Hartwell to Bowersville	10	1879		
(1)Richmond & Danville						
(2)Southern						
LAWRENCEVILLE BRANCH	3'	Lawrenceville to Suwanee	10	1881		
(1)Richmond & Danville						
(2)S.--Atlantic & Charlotte Air Line Ry. (190)						
MARIETTA & N. GEORGIA	3'	Marietta to Murphy	109	1884	1886	
(1)Atlanta Knoxville & No. (1896)						
(2)L.&N.						
MEMPHIS BRANCH	3'	Rome to Terminus	5	1873		1893
OCMULGEE RIVER & NORMANDALE	3'6"	Normandale to Ocmulgee River	29			
ROSWELL	3'	Roswell to Roswell Jct.	9.25	1881		
(1)Richmond & Danville						
(2)Southern						
WALTON	3'	Monroe to Social Circle	10			
(1)Ga. Ry & Banking Co. (1889)						

IDAHO

NAME	GGE.	TERMINI	MILES	BUILT	S.G.	ABD.
COEUR D'ALENE RY. & NAV.	3'	Mission to State Line	44.52	1887	1897	
		Wallace to Burke	7.87			
(1)N.P. (1897)						

ILLINOIS

NAME	GGE.	TERMINI	MILES	BUILT	S.G.	ABD.
CAIRO & EAST ST. LOUIS	3'	Cairo to East St. Louis	146.5	1875	1883	
(1)St. Louis & Cairo (1882)						
(2)Mobile & Ohio						
DANVILLE OLNEY & OHIO RIV.	3'	Kansas to Westfield	8	1878	.1881	
(1)Chicago & Ohio Riv. (1886)						
(2)Peoria Decatur & Evansville (1893)						
(3)Illinois Central						
FULTON COUNTY EXT. RY.	3'	Fairview to Galesburg	31.3	1882	1905	193-
(1)C.B.&Q.						
FULTON COUNTY N. G.	3'	Galesburg to West Havana	61	1880	1905	193-
(1)C.B.&Q.						
HAVANA RANTOUL & E.	3'	West Lebanon, Ind. to LeRoy Ill.	75.67	1879	1887	
(A)Mississippi & Atlantic						
(A)LeRoy Narrow Gauge						
(1)Rantoul						
(2)Illinois Central						

ILLINOIS

NAME	GGE.	TERMINI	MILES	BUILT	S.G.	ABD.
IND. & ILL. SO. RY. (1886)	3'	Switz City, Ind. to Effingham, Ill.	90		1887	
(A)Springfield, Effingham &						
So.East Ry.				1880		
(A)Bloomfield						
(1)St. Louis Ind. & E. (1890)						
(2)Illinois & Indiana						
MOLINE & S.E.	3'6"	Moline to Cool Valley	8	1879		1888

INDIANA

NAME	GGE.	TERMINI	MILES	BUILT	S.G.	ABD.
BEDFORD SPRINGVILLE						
OWENSBURG & BLOOMFIELD	3'	Bedford to Switz City	42.86	1876	1883	
(1)Bedford & Bloomfield						
(1)Louisville N. Albany &						
Chicago (1886)						
(2)Chi. Indianapolis Louisville						
(1879)						
INDIANAPOLIS DELPHI & CHI.	3'	Rennselaer to Delphi	40	1879	1887	
(1)Illinois Central (1886)						

IOWA

NAME	GGE.	TERMINI	MILES	BUILT	S.G.	ABD.
BURLINGTON & N.W. RY.	3'	Burlington to Washington	52.0	1880		
(1)C.B.&Q.						
BURLINGTON & WESTERN	3'	Winfield to Oskaloosa	70.70	1884		
(A)Burl. Cedar River & No.		Burlington to Winfield	33.8			
(1)Burlington N.W.						
(2)C.B.&Q.						
CROOKED CREEK RY.	3'	Lehigh to Judd	8.5	1876	1887	
DES MOINES - ADEL & W.	3'	Waukee to Pervia	28.5	1879	1892	
(1)Des Moines N.W. (1880)						
(2)Wabash St. Louis & Pac.						
(3)Wabash						
DES MOINES & MINNEAPOLIS	3'	Des Moines to Callanan	56.73	1878	1880	
(A)Des Moines & Minnesota						
(1)C.&N.W. (1879)						
DES MOINES OSCEDA & SO.	3'	Des Moines to Cainsville, Mo.	111.9	1885	1897	
(1)Des M. & Kansas City						
(1887)						
FARMERS UNION	3'	Liscomb & Beaman	12	1875		
FT. MADISON & N.W. RY.	3'	Ft. Madison to Birmingham	45	1885	1892	
(1)Chi. Ft. Madison & Des						
Moines Ry. (1890)						
IOWA EASTERN	3'	Beulah to Stultah	15	1877	1882	
(1)C.M.&St.P. (1882)						
ST. LOUIS DES MOINES & N. RY.	3'	Des Moines to Boone	42.37	1882	1891	
(1)Des Moines & N. (1889)						
(2)Des Moines N. & W. (1891)						
ST. LOUIS KEOSAUQUA & ST.						
PAUL	3'	Keosauqua to Summit	4			
WAUKON & MISSISSIPPI	3'	Waukon Junction to Waukon	23	1877	1880	
(1)C.M.&St.P. (1880)						

KANSAS

NAME	GGE.	TERMINI	MILES	BUILT	S.G.	ABD.
CAMPBELL & ST. FRANCIS						
VALLEY RY.	3'	Campbell to Buckhorn	20		1910	
		Campbell to Webbers Mill	5			
(1)St. Louis Kennett & S.E.						
(1906)						
KANSAS CENTRAL	3'	Leavenworth to Miltonville	165.35	1877	1891	
(1)Leavenworth Kansas & W.						
(1897)						
(2)U.P.						
MEMPHIS KANSAS & COLO. RY.	3'	Weir City to Cherryvale	49.79	1881	1882	
(1)Kansas City Ft. Scott &						
Gulf						
(2)Kansas City Ft. Scott &						
Memphis						
(3)St. Louis S. W.						

KENTUCKY

NAME	GGE.	TERMINI	MILES	BUILT	S.G.	ABD.
COVINGTON FLEMINGSBURG &						
POUND GAP	3'	Johnston to Hillsboro	18	1878	1882	
(A)Covington Flemingsburg &						
Ashland (1903)						
(1)Licking Valley Ry. (1879)						
(2)Cincinnati & S. E. (1880)						
KENTUCKY & S. ATLANTIC	3'	Mount Sterling to Rothwell	19.8	1876	1895	
(A)Mt. Sterling (1881)						
(1)C.&O.						

KENTUCKY

NAME	GGE.	TERMINI	MILES	BUILT	S.G.	ABD.
LICKING RIVER	3'	Salt Lick to Blackwater	33	1898		1913
(A)Licking Valley (1897)						
LOUISVILLE, HARROD CREEK						
& WESTPORT	3'	Louisville to Prospect	11	1875	1888	
(1)L.& N. (1881)						
MOUNTAIN CENTRAL RY.	3'	Campton Jct. to Campton	12			
		Chimneytop Branch	7			
PINE HILL	3'		3			
RED RIVER VALLEY	3'	Rothwell to McCausey	9	1903		1914

LOUISIANA

NAME	GGE.	TERMINI	MILES	BUILT	S.G.	ABD.
BODCAW VALLEY	3'	Alden Bridge to Ivan	18	1905		1913
HOUSTON & SHREVEPORT (1891)	3'	Shreveport to Logansport	40		1894	
(A)Shreveport & Houston				1886		
(1)Houston E. & W. Texas						
(2)S. P. Co. (1890)						
KENTWOOD & EAST	3'	Kentwood to Hackley	31	1905		
KENTWOOD GREENSBURG						
& SOUTH WEST	3'	Kents Mill to Freiler	14.20	1906		
LAKE CHARLES & LEESVILLE	3'	Banks to Bundicks	38			
MARTINDALE & OUACHITA						
RIVER RY.	3'	Bolinger to Bodcaw	10	1898		
		Bolinger to Burgess	7			
NATCHEZ RED RIVER & TEXAS	3'	Vidalia to Black River	25	1886	1907	
(A)Vidalia Western						
(1)Natchez & Western (1904)						
(2)St. Louis Iron Mt. & So.						
OLD RIVER & KISSATCHIE RY		Old River to Jerguson	26			
WHITE CASTLE & LAKE						
NATCHEZ			10			
ZIMMERMAN LEESVILLE & S.W.		Zimmerman to Edwards	19			
		Odum Jct. to Hoyt	3			

MAINE

NAME	GGE.	TERMINI	MILES	BUILT	S.G.	ABD.
AROOSTOOK RIVER	3'6"	Caribou to New Brunswick Line	15	1876		
		Presque Isle to Caribou	15	1881		
(1)Canadian Pacific						
BRIDGTON & SACO. RIVER	2'	Harrison to Bridgton Jct.	22.75	1883		1930
BRIDGTON & HARRISON	2'	Bridgton Jct. to Bridgton	18	1930		1940
EUSTIS	2'	Eustis Jct. to Berlin Mill	15	1903		1909
KENNEBEC CENTRAL	2'	Randolph to Togus	5	1890		1929
MONSON	2'	Monson Jct. to Monson	6	1883		1939
		Monson to Slate Quarries	2			
SANDY RIVER & RANGELEY						
LAKES (1908)						
Franklin & Megantic	2'	Strong to Bigelow	31	1897		1936
Kingfield & Dead River	2'	Kingfield to Carabasset	81	1894		
Madrid	2'	Madrid Station to #6	15.4	1902		
Phillips & Rangeley	2'	Phillips to Rangeley	29	1891		
Sandy River	2'	Farmington to Phillips	18	1879		
WISCASSET WATERVILLE &						
FARMINGTON RY.	2'	Wiscasset to Winslow	43	1901		
		Weeks Mills Jct. to Albion	15.26			
(A)Wiscasset & Quebec						
(1)Wiscasset Waterville &						
Farmington (1909)		Wiscasset to Albin				1932

MARYLAND

NAME	GGE.	TERMINI	MILES	BUILT	S.G.	ABD.
MARYLAND CENTRAL RY.	3'	Baltimore to Delta, Pa.	44.4	(1888)	1891	
(A)Maryland Central	3'	Baltimore to Baldwin & Delta		1884		
(A)Baltimore & Delta	3'	Baltimore to Loch Raven	19	1882		
Slate Ridge & Delta	3'	Slate Ridge to Delta, Pa.	1			
York & Peach Bottom	3'	York, Pa. to Peach Bottom	40	1874		
(1)Maryland & Penn. (1901)						

MASSACHUSETTS

NAME	GGE.	TERMINI	MILES	BUILT	S.G.	ABD.
BILLERICA & BEDFORD	2'	North Billerica to Bedford Mass.	8.63	1877		1878
BOSTON REVERE BEACH &						
LYNN	3'	East Boston to Lynn	8.8	1875		1938
(A)Boston Winthrop & Shore						
(Con 1891)		Boston to Winthrop	4.4	1883		
Eastern Jct.						
Broad Sound Pier & Pt. Shirley						
Boston Winthrop & Pt. Shirley						
Boston & Winthrop						
DEERFIELD RIVER	3'	Hoosac Tunnel to Sherman Sta.				
		Vermont.	8	1885		
(1)Hoosac Tunnel &						
Wilmington (1894)						

MASSACHUSETTS

NAME	GGE.	TERMINI	MILES	BUILT	S.G.	ABD.
GRAFTON CENTRE	3'	Grafton to Grafton Centre	3	1874	1887	
(1)Grafton & Upton (Elect)						
MARTHAS VINEYARD	3'	Cottage City to Katama & S. Beach	8.78	1874		1896
NANTUCKET	3'	Nantucket to Siasconsett	11.16	1884		1910
(1)Nantucket Central (1895)						
WORCESTER & SHREWSBURY	3'	Worcester to Lake Quinsigamond	2.7	1873	189-	

MICHIGAN

NAME	GGE.	TERMINI	MILES	BUILT	S.G.	ABD.
AU SABLE & N. W. RY.	3'	Au Sable to Red Oak	50.68	1889	1914	
(1)Detroit & Mackinac (1914)						
BEAR LAKE & EAST	3'	Pierport to Springdale	16	1887		1902
BUCKLEY & DOUGLAS	3'	Manistee River - N.E.	10	1881		1888
HANCOCK & CALUMET	3'	Hancock to End of Line	26.74	1886	1901	
		Jct. to Lake Linden		1885		
(1)Mineral Range						
HARBOR SPRING	2'6"	Harbor Spring to Carters Mill	8	1902		1910
HECLA & TORCH LAKE	4'1"	Hecla Mine to Lake Linden	7	1868		1908
HOBART & MANISTEE RIVER	3'	Hobart to Manistee River	9.24	1879		1890
JACKSON & NO.	3'	Jackson to Portage	4		1909	1911
LAC LA BELLE & CALUMET	3'	Lac La Belle to Delaware Mine	7.63	1883		1888
LAKE HURON & S. W.	3'	Towas City to Camp Watson	13			1902
LEWISTON & S. E.	3'	Lewiston to Forest Terminus	15	1896		1911
MANISTEE & LUTHER	3'	Eastlake to End of Track	45			1914
(A)Chippewa Valley				1886		
MASON & OCEANA	3'	Ludington to Beaver	35	1901	1909	
MINERAL RANGE	3'	Franklin Sta. to Quincy Mine	2.20	1885	1901	
MUSKRAT LAKE & CLAM RIV.	3'	Muskrat Lake to Clam River	8	1882		1893
PAW PAW	3'	Lawton to Paw Paw	4	(S.G. 1867 N.G. 1875)		1904
(1)Toledo & S. Haven (1887)						
PORT HURON & N.W. RY.	3'	Port Huron to Saginaw	91	1882	1889	
		Saginaw Jct. to Sand	58.25			
		Port Austin to Palms	35	1882		
		Port Huron to Almont	38.75	1882		
(1)Flint & Pere Marquette (1890)						
QUINCY & TORCH LAKE	3'	Quincy Mine to Quincy Stamp Mill	6	1890		
RED RIVER VALLEY	3'	Rothwell to Apperson	14			1912
SAGINAW & MT PLEASANT	3'	East Saginaw to Mt. Pleasant	14.51	1879	1880	
(1)Flint & Pere Marquette (1880)						
SAGINAW TUSCOLA & HURON		East Saginaw to Bad Axe	64.38	1882	1891	
		Jct. to Quincy	8.81			
		Bay Port Jct. to Bay Port		1883		
(1)Pere Marquette						
ST. JOSEPH VALLEY	3'	Buchanan to Berrien Springs	10	1881	1889	
(1)St. Joseph Vy. Ry. (1889)						
(2)Milwaukee Benton Harbor & Columbus (1897)						
TOLEDO & S. HAVEN	3'	Paw Paw to Lawrence	9	1857	1899	
(1)So. Haven & Eastern (1894)						
TOWAS & BAY COUNTY	3'2"	Towas City to 5 miles beyond Camp	8	1881	1886	
(1)Detroit Bay City & Alpina (1883)						
(2)Detroit & Mackinac (1894)						
WEST BRANCH & MOORESTOWN	3'	Moorestown to Muskegon River	10.5	1882		1891

MINNESOTA

NAME	GGE.	TERMINI	MILES	BUILT	S.G.	ABD.
MINNEAPOLIS-LYNDALE & MINNETONKA RY.	3'	Minneapolis to Excelsior	20	1882		
(A)Minneapolis Minnehaha & Ft. Snelling Ry.	3'	Minneapolis to Minnehaha Falls	4.24	1884	1887	1934
(1)Minn. ST. Ry. Co. (1887)						
(2)Minn. & St. Paul Suburban						
MINNESOTA MIDLAND	3'	Wabasha to Zumbrote	60	1878	1883	
(1)C.M.&St. P. (1883)						

MISSISSIPPI

NAME	GGE.	TERMINI	MILES	BUILT	S.G.	ABD.
GREENVILLE COLUMBUS & BIRMINGHAM	3'	Greenville to Johnsonville & Arcola	40	1877	1894	
(1)Georgia Pacific (1881)						
(2)Southern (1894)						
KINGSTON & CENTRAL MISS.	3'	Laurel to Bay Springs	25	1901	1904	
(1)Mobile Jackson & K. C.						
LIBERTY WHITE	3'	McComb City to Keiths	17.6	1904		1921

MISSISSIPPI

NAME	GGE.	TERMINI	MILES	BUILT	S.G.	ABD.
MISS. VALLEY & SHIP ISLAND	3'6"	Vicksburg to Morehead	26	1872	1906	
(1)Louisville New Orleans & Texas (1884)						
(2)Mobile Jackson & K. C.						
MOBILE & N. W.	3'	Glendale to Clarksville	31	1879	1890	
(1)Louisville New Orleans & Texas						
(2)Yazoo & Mississippi Valley (1892)						
NATCHEZ JACKSON & COLUMBUS	3'6"	Natchez to Jackson	98.6	1882	'89-90	
(1)Louisville New Orleans & Texas (1889)						
(2)Yazoo & Miss. Vy. (1892)						
NATCHEZ RED RIV. & TEXAS	3'	Vidalia to Black River	25	1886		
(1)Natchez & W. Ry. (1904)						
SHIP ISLAND RIPLEY & KENTUCKY (1888)	3'	Middleton, Tenn. to Ripley, Miss.	25	1872	189-	
(A)Ripley						
(1)Gulf & Chicago (1889)		Nor. Div. Gulf & Ship Island, Ripley to Pontotoc	37			
(2)Mobile Jackson & K. C.						
VICKSBURG & NASHVILLE	3'	Grenada to Mile Post 5	5			1872
(A)Grenada Houston & East				1871		

MISSOURI

NAME	GGE.	TERMINI	MILES	BUILT	S.G.	ABD.
KANSAS CITY & E. (1878)	3'	Kansas City to Lexington	43	1876	1881	
(A)Wyandotte K. C. & N.W.						
(1)Missouri Pacific (1880)						
LITTLE RIVER VALLEY & ARK.	3'	New Madrid to Malden	27.1	1878	1887	
(1)St. Louis Ark. & Texas						
MILL SPRING CURRENT RIV. & BARNESVILLE	3'	Leeper to Ellington	37	1886	1907	
(1)Missouri S. (1857)						
MISS. RIV. & BONNE TERRE RY.	3'	Bonne Terre to Riverside	31.68	1890	1894	
POPLAR BLUFF & DAN RIVER	3'10"	Poplar Bluff to Rushville	15			
SEDALIA WARSAW & S. RY.	3'	Sedalia to Warsaw	42.25	1880	1881	
(1)Sedalia Warsaw & S. W.						
(2)Missouri Pacific (1881)						
ST. JOSEPH & DESLOGE RY.	3'	Bonne Terre to Summit	13	1880		1918
(1)St. Joseph Ry. (1886)						
ST. JOSEPH & DES MOINES	3'	St. Joseph to Albany	50	1878	1886	
(1)C.B. & Q. (1882)						
ST. LOUIS CREVE COEUR & ST. CHARLES RY.	3'	Grand Ave St. L. to Florissant	18		1890	
(A)West End Narrow Gauge				1878	(4 10)	
(1)St. L. Cable & W. Ry. Co. (1884)						
(2)St. Louis Suburban						

MONTANA

NAME	GGE.	TERMINI	MILES	BUILT	S.G.	ABD.
MONTANA SOUTHERN	3'	Divide Southward	40	1918		1924

NEBRASKA

NAME	GGE.	TERMINI	MILES	BUILT	S.G.	ABD.
COVINGTON COLUMBUS & BLACK HILLS	3'6"	Covington to Ponca	26	1876	1880	
(1)St. Paul & Sioux City (1879)						
(2)C. St. P. M. & O. (1880)						

NEVADA

NAME	GGE.	TERMINI	MILES	BUILT	S.G.	ABD.
AUSTIN CITY	3'	Nev. Cent. sta. thru Austin	2.5	1880		
BATTLE MOUNTAIN & LEWIS	3'	Lewis Jct. to Lewis	5	1881		1882
CARSON & COLORADO	3'	Mound House to Churchill	26.3	1881	1905	1934
(1)Nev. & Cal. (SP) (1900)		Churchill to Hawthorne	69.5	1882	1905	
		Hawthorne by-pass built		1905		
		Mina to Tonopah Jct.	9	1882	1905	1949
		Ton. Jct. to Benton, Cal.	49.7	'82-83		1938
		Benton to Laws, Cal.	30.65	1883		1943
		Laws to Keeler, Cal.	71.33	1883		
		Cottonwood Branch	7.3	1891		1902
		Candelaria Branch	5.5	1882		1932
CRYSTAL BAY (op. by C&T Lbr. & Flum.)	3'	At L. Tahoe, Washoe Co.	11			1895
EUREKA & PALISADE	3'	Palisade to Eureka	84	1876		1938
(1)Eureka Nev. 1912.						
(2)Op. by Nev. Trans. Co. (1912)						

NEVADA

NAME	GGE.	TERMINI	MILES	BUILT	S.G.	ABD.
LAKE TAHOE (op. by C&T Lbr. & Flum.)	3'	Glenbrook to Summit	10	1875		1898
GOLCONDA & ADELAIDE	3'	Golconda to Adelaide	11	1895		1915
(1)Glasgow & Adelaide						
NEVADA, CALIF. & OREGON	3'	(See under "California")				
NEVADA CENTRAL	3'	Battle Mtn. to Austin	93.5	1880		1938
NEVADA SHORT LINE	3'	Oreana to Rochester	12	1916		1919
PIOCHE & BULLIONVILLE	3'	Pioche to Bullionville	21.25	187-		
PIOCHE PACIFIC	3'	Pioche westward to mines.	15			
(A)Pacific Trans. Co.(1901)						
(1)Bristol Silver Mines						1948
RUBY HILL						
(1)Eureka Nevada 1911	3'	Eureka to Ruby Hill	7 4	Partial aband.		1894
TONOPAH	3'	Tonopah Jct. to Tonopah	60	1903	1905	1948
(1)Tonopah & Goldfield (1905)		Ton. Jct. to Mina (over SP)	9		1905	1949

NEW HAMPSHIRE

NAME	GGE.	TERMINI	MILES	BUILT	S.G.	ABD.
PROFILE & FRANCONIA NOTCH	3'	Profile House to Bethlehem	12.84	1879	1894-5	1927
(1)Concord & Montreal (1901)						
(2)Boston & Maine						

NEW JERSEY

NAME	GGE.	TERMINI	MILES	BUILT	S.G.	ABD.
CAMDEN GLOUCESTER & MT. EPHRIAM RY.	3'		5.97	1878	1889	
(1)Atlantic City (1889)						
FERRO MONTE.	2'10"	Vanaha Station to Byram Mine	2.54	1870		1892
PHILADELPHIA & ATL. CITY	3'6"	Camden to Atlantic City		1877	1885	
(1)Atlantic City						

NEW MEXICO

NAME	GGE.	TERMINI	MILES	BUILT	S.G.	ABD.
RIO GRANDE & SOUTHWESTERN	3'	Lumberton to Gallina	42	1904		
(1)D&RG *N*						
SANTA FE S. RY. (1888)	3'	Santa Fe to Espanola	29.5	1886		1941
(A)Texas S. Fe & No. Ry.						
(1)Rio Grande & S. Fe. (1895)						
(2)D. & R. G. (1897)						
SILVER CITY, DEMING & PAC.	3'	Deming to Silver City	48.29	1883	1884	
(1)A. T. & S. F.						
SILVER CITY, PINOS ALTOS & MOGOLLON	2'	Silver City to Pinos Altos	16	1906		1913
TIERRA AMARILLA & S.	3'	Chama to Tierra Amarilla				1903

NEW YORK

NAME	GGE.	TERMINI	MILES	BUILT	S.G.	ABD.
ADDISON & N. PENN. RY.	3'	Addison, N.Y. to Gaines, Pa.	41	1882	1893	
		Jct. to Gurnee, Pa.	4.5	1883		
(1)Addison & Penn. (1887)						
(2)Add. & Susquehanna (1898)						
(3)Buffalo & Susquehanna (1901)						
ALLEGANY CENTRAL	3'	Olean to Swains	58.89	1882	'83-01	
(1)Lackawanna & Pitts.(1883)						
(2)Lackawanna & S.W. (1889)						
(3)Central N.Y. & W. (1892)						
(4)Pitts. Shawmut & N. (1889)						
BATH & HAMMONDSPORT	3'	Bath to Hammondsport	9.8	1875	1890	
BRADFORD ELDRED & CUBA	3'	Little Genesee to Ceres	4.31	1882		1893
		Cuba to Little Genesee		1882		1889
Bradford Richburg & Cuba	3'	Eldred Pa. to Ceres	9.36	1881		1893
Wellsville Bolivar & Eldred	3'	Wellsville to Little Genesee	19.07	1882		1893
		Bolivar to Richburg	1.5			
CATSKILL MOUNTAIN	3'	Catskill to Palenville	15.75	1882		1919
(A)Cairo	3'	Cairo to Cairo Jct.	3.77	1884		1919
(1)Catskill Mt. Ry. (1885)						
(2)Catskill Mt. R.R. Corp.(1917)						
CATSKILL & TANNERSVILLE RY.	3'	Otis Summit to Tannersville	6	1893		1919
(1)Catskill Mt. R.R. Corp.(1917)						
CHATEAUGAY	3'	Dannemora to Lyon Mountain	18.01	1880	1903	
Chateaugay Ry.	3'	Lyon Mt. to Saranac Lake	38.89	1888		
Saranac & Lake Placid	3'	Saranac to Lake Placid	9.93	1893		
Plattsburgh to Dannemora (Dannemora)	3'	Plattsburgh to Dannemora		1879		
(1)Chateaugay & Lake Placid (1903)						
(2)Delaware & Hudson						

NEW YORK

NAME	GGE	TERMINI	MILES	BUILT	S.G.	ABD.
CROWN PT. IRON COMPANY	3'	Crown Pt. to Hammondsville	13	1874	1881	1898
HAYTS CORNERS OVID & WILLARD	3'	Hayts Corner to Willard	3.83	1883	1890	
(1)Geneva Ithaca & Sayre (1883)						
(2)Lehigh Valley (1889)						
HERKIMER NEWPORT & POLAND	3'6"	Herkimer to Poland	16.73	1882	1892	
(1)Mohawk & Molone (1892)						
(2)N.Y. Central & Hudson River (1893)						
KAATERSKILL	3'	Kaaterskill Jct. to Kaa. Station	7.5	1883	1902	
(1)Ulster & Delaware (1900)						
MARINE RY.	3'	Manhattan Beach to Sheepshead Bay Inlet	2	1878	1883	
		Man. Beach Hotel to Brighton Beach	.5			
N.Y. & MANHATTAN BEACH	3'	Greenpoint to Man. Beach	14.79	1877	1882	
(A)N.Y. Bay Ridge & Jamacia.	3'	Bay Ridge to New Lots	8.16	1877		
(A)Glendale & East River	3'	Greenpoint to Cooper Ave.	2.70	1878		
(1)L. I. (1885)						
OTIS RY.	3'	Otis Jct. to Otis Summit	1.35	1892		1919
(A)Otis Elevating Ry. Catskill Mt. R.R. Corp. (1917)						
ROCHESTER & GLEN HAVEN	3'	Rochester to Glen Haven	3.5	1889	1896	
(1)Glen Haven (1893)						
(2)Irondequoit Park Ry. (1895)						
SARATOGA MOUNT McGREGOR & LAKE GEORGE	3'	Saratoga Springs to Mt. McGregor	10.5	1883		1900
(1)Mt. McGregor (1889)						
(2)Saratoga & Mt. McGregor (1896)						
(3)Saratoga Northern (1897)						
SPRINGVILLE & SARDINIA	3'	Springville to Sardinia	11.57	1878		1886
STONEY CLOVE & CATSKILL MOUNTAIN	3'	Phoenicia to Hunter	14.3	1882	1900	
(1)Ulster & Delaware (1893)						
TONAWANDA VALLEY & CUBA	3'	Attica to Freedom	33	1882	1895	
(1)Attica & Freedom (1891)						
(2)Buffalo Attica & Arcade (1894)						
(3)Erie						

NORTH CAROLINA

NAME	GGE	TERMINI	MILES	BUILT	S.G.	ABD.
CALDWELL & NORTHERN	3	Lenoir to Collettsville	10	1895	1906	
CASHIE & CHOWAN R.R. & LUMBER CO.	3'6"	Howard to Swamps	30	1883		1913
CASHIE & ROANOKE	3'	Wellington to Powellsville	22	1898		
(1)Wellington & Powellsville (1893)						
DANVILLE MACKSVILLE & S.W.	3'	Danville to Mooresville		1882	1900	
(1)Danville & New River						
(2)Danville & W. (1890)						
LAUREL RIVER & HOT SPRINGS	2'	Hot Springs to 3 Miles North	3	1892		1893
LAWNDALE RY.	3'	Lawndale to Lawndale Jct.	9.06	1899		1945
(1)Lawndale Ry. & Industrial		Lawndale Jct. to Shelby	2.4			
LINVILLE RIVER RY.	3'6"	Pineola to Cranberry	12	1902		1941
MT. AIRY & EASTERN	3'	Mt. Airy Jct. to Danube, Va.	19.25	1900		1918
RED SPRINGS & BOWMORE	3'	Red Springs to Wagrom	16	1902		1918
WASHINGTON & PLYMOUTH	3'	Washington to Plymouth	33	1902	1905	
(1)Norfolk Sou. (1904)						
WINTON R.R. & LUMBER CO.	4'	St. Johns to Winton	15	1890		1902

OHIO

NAME	GGE	TERMINI	MILES	BUILT	S.G.	ABD.
ALLIANCE & LAKE ERIE	3	Alliance to Phalanx	23.3	1879	1887	
(1)Lake Erie Alli. & S. (1886)						
(2)Ohio Riv. & Lake Erie (1895)						
BELLAIRE ZANESVILLE & CINCINNATI RY. (1882)	3					
(A)Bellaire & Southwestern	3'	Bellaire to Woodsfield	42	1879	1898	
(A)Zanesville & Southeastern	3'	Bellaire to Zanesville	112	1882		
(1)Ohio River & Western						
CHAGRIN FALLS & SOUTHERN	3'	Chagrin Falls to Solon	8	1882	1893	
(A)Painesville Canton & Bridgeport						
(1)Cleveland Chagrin Fls. & N.						
(2)Clev. Canton & S. (1893)						

OHIO

NAME	GGE.	TERMINI	MILES	BUILT	S.G.	ABD.
CINCINNATI ATL. & COLUMBUS	3'	Milford to Newtonville	11	1883		1891
(A)Cin. Columbus & Huntington						
CINCINNATI & EASTERN	3'	Idlewild to Wharton	99.1	1877	1884	
		Jct. to New Richmond	14.8			
(1)Ohio & N.W. (1887)						
(2)Cin. Portsmouth & Va. (1890)						
(3)Norfolk & W. (1901)						
CINCINNATI LEBANON & N. RY.	3'	Cincinnati to Dodds	36.25	1885	1894	
		Blue Ash to Montgomery	1.4			
(1)Pennsylvania (1896)						
CINCINNATI & PORTSMOUTH	3'	Cincinnati to Amelia		1877	1902	
(1)Cin. Georgetown & Ports.		Cincinnati to Georgetown	42	1886		
(2)Cin., Georgetown (1928)						
CINCINNATI & WESTWOOD	3'	Cincinnati to Robbs Station	5.63	1876	189-	
CLEVELAND & WESTERN	3'	Delphos to Carey	56	1886		
(A)Cleveland Delphos & St. L.				1882		
COLLEGE HILL	3'	College Hill Jct. to Mt. Healthy	6.5	1877	1885	
(1)Cincinnati N.W. (1883)						
COLUMBUS & MAYSVILLE	3'	Hillsboro & Sardinia	18.7	1877	1887	
(A)Hillsboro Short Line	3'	Jct. M. & C. to Hillsboro	1.9			
(1)Ohio & N.W. (1887)						
CONNOTTON VALLEY RY.	3'	Cleveland to Coshocton	115.13	1881	1888	
(A)Ohio & Toledo (1874)		Canton to Sharrodville	42.76			
(A)Youngstown & Conn. (1878)		Oneida to Minerva	2.70			
(1)Clev. & Canton (1885)						
(2)Clev. Canton & S. (1892)						
(3)W. & L.E. (1899)						
DAYTON COVINGTON & TOLEDO	3'	Jct. to Versailles	35			
DAYTON & IRONTON	3'	Dayton to Delphos	95.7		1884	
		Buckeye Branch	2			
(A)Dayton & S.E. (1879)						
(A)Toledo Delphos & Burlington (1879)						
(A)Toledo Cincinnati & St. L.						
(1)Dayton Ft. Wayne & Chicago (1887)						
(2)Cin. Dayton & Chi. (1893)						
(3)Cin. Hamilton & Day.(1895)						
PITTSBURGH PAINESVILLE & FAIRPORT	3'	Fairport to Youngstown	62.3			
(A)Painesville & Youngstown				1874	1886	
(1)Pitts. Cleveland & Toledo (1882)		Fairport to Niles.				
(2)Pittsburg & W. (1886)						
(3)B. & O.						
SPRINGFIELD SOUTHERN	3'	Springfield to Wellston	118.25	1878	1882	
(A)Springfield Jackson & Pomeroy (1878)						
(1)Ohio Southern (1881)						
(2)Detroit Southern (1900)						
ST. CLAIRSVILLE	3'	Quincy to St. Clairsville	6.5	1877	1888	
(1)Bellaire & St. Cla. (1885)						
(2)Ohio Central (1888)						
TOLEDO CINCINNATI & ST. L.	3'	Toledo to East St. Louis Ill.	449.67	Dissolved 1884		
(A)Toledo & Maumee. (1874)		Delphos to Buckeye Furnace	219.08			
		Ironton Jct. to Ironton	54.21			
		Lebanon to Dodds	16.82			
		Dodds Jct. to Cincinnati	37.40			
(1)Cincinnati Lebanon & N.	3'	Cincinnati to Dodds	36	1884	1894	
(1)Pennsylvania						
TRUMBULL & MAHONING	3'	Niles to Youngstown	10		1905	
(A)Rem. of Pitts. Painesville & Fairport (1886)						
(1)B. & O.						

OREGON

NAME	GGE.	TERMINI	MILES	BUILT	S.G.	ABD.
DAYTON, SHERIDAN & GRAND RONDE	3'	Dayton to Dallas & Junction	35	1878		
(1)Willamette Vy. Ry. (1880)						
(2)Oregon Ry. (1880)						
(3)Oregonian Ry., as below						
OREGONIAN RY.	3'	Fulquartz to Airlie				
(A)See above		Lafayette to Dundee	55.7	1881	1893	
		Rays Landing to Coburg	89.7	1882	1893	
		Sheridan Jct. to Ballston	4.3	1882		

OREGON

NAME	GGE.	TERMINI	MILES	BUILT	S.G.	ABD.
(1)Ore. Ry. & Nav.(1881-1884)						
(2)Southern Pacific (1893)						
OREGON STATE PORTAGE	3'	Cascades of Columbia River	3	1891	1896	
PORTLAND & VANCOUVER	3'	Portland to Vancouver, Wash.	7			
(1)Portland Consol. St. Ry., Port. St. Ry., Port. Ry. Lt. & Pwr., PNWPS, Portland Traction. Electrified in 1893.						
PORTLAND & WILLAMETTE VALLEY	3'	Portland to Dundee Jct.	28.5	1887	1892	
		S. Portland to Ore. Steel Works	2.6			
(1)Portland & Yamhill						
(2)Southern Pacific (1892)						
SUMPTER VALLEY	3'	Baker to McEwen	25	1892		1946
		. . .extended to Sumpter	10	1896		
		. . .extended to Whitney	14	1899		
		. . .extended to Austin	13.2	1905		
		. . .extended to Prairie City	20	1911		1932

PENNSYLVANIA

NAME	GGE.	TERMINI	MILES	BUILT	S.G.	ABD.
ALTOONA & BEECH CREEK	3'	Altoona to Fallen Timber	18			
(1)Altoona Juniata & N. (1910)						
(2)Altoona N. (1913)						
BELLS GAP	3'	Bellwood to Irvona	25.4	1873	1890	
(1)Pennsylvania & N.W.						
BIG LEVEL & KINUZA						
(1)Pittsburgh W. (1911)						
BRADFORD, BORDELL & KINZUA						
Bradford Ry.	3'	Bradford to Jct. with Kinzua	14	1881		
Bradford Bordell & Smethport	3'	Simpson to Smethport	10.23	1880		
Big Level & Kinzua	3'	Mt. Jewett to Ormsby	10.7	1886		
Kendall & Eldred	3'	Eldred to Tarpot	18.28	1877		1898
Kinzua	3'	Jct. with Bradford Ry. to Kinzua	14.04		1899	
Rew City & Eldred	3'	Rew City to Eldred	12.16	1882		1893
Olean Bradford & Warren	3'	Olean N.Y. to Penn. State Line	12.53	1878	1900	
Olean Bradford & Warren Ry.	3'	Penn. State Line to Bradford	14	1878	1900	
(1)W. N.Y. & Pennsylvania						
(2)Pennsylvania						
BRADFORD & W. PENN.	3'	Lewis Run to Big Camp	6.5	1895		1913
(1)Lewis Run Mfg. Co.						
COUDERSPORT & PORT ALLEGANY	3'	Port Allegany to Coudersport	17.	1882	1889	
EAGLES MERE	3'	Sonestown to Eagles Mere	8	1892		1927
EAST BOARD TOP	3'	Mt. Union to Robertsdale	30	1874		
EVERGREEN RY.	3'	Bennett to Brookfield	4	1882		
(A)Lawrenceville & Evergreen	3'	Bennett to Evergreen	2.61	1873		1909
(1)Pittsburgh & N. Ry. (1887)						
(2)Baltimore & Ohio						
GREENLICK N.G. RY.	3'	Greenlick Jct. to Mt. Vernon Mines	3.5	1875		1903
KEYSTONE COAL CO.	3'	Keystone Jct. to Keystone Mines	5.5	1877		1895
LANCASTER OXFORD & S.	3'	Oxford to Peach Bottom	20	(1890)		
		Fairmount to Quarryville	8	1906		
(A)Peach Bottom	3'	Oxford to Dorseys	20	1874		
LIGONIER VALLEY	3'	Latrobe to Ligonier	10.5	1877	1882	
LITTLE SAW MILL RUN	3'	Pittsburg to Banksville	3	(S.G. 1853 N.G. 1878 S.G. 1889)		
(1)W. Side Belt (1897)						
MONTROSE	3'	Montrose to Tunkhannock	28	1873		
(1)Lehigh Valley						
MT. GRETNA N.G. RY.	2'	Mt. Gretna Port to Gov. Dick	4	1889		1916
MT. JEWETT KINZUA & RITERSVILLE	3'	Mt. Jewett to Doyles	5	1889	1892	
NEW CASTLE	3'6"	New Castle to Coal Centre	5.5	1872		1890
NEW CASTLE & BUTLER	3'	New Castle to Mineral Ridge	2.5	1881		1919
NEWPORT & SHERMANS VY.	3'	Newport to New Germantown	28.5	1892		1923
PITTS. & CASTLE SHANNON	3'4'	Pittsburg to Arlington	7	1871		
PITTSBURG SO. N.G.	3'	Pittsburg to Washington	36.5	1879	1882	
(1)Baltimore & Ohio						
PITTS. & W. (1883) STD. G. PRIOR TO 1915						
Emlenton Shipp. & Clarion	3'	Emlenton to Clarion	29.7	1877		
Foxburg St. Peter. & Clarion	3'	Foxburg to Jefferson	12.20	1877	1900	
Karns City & Butler	3'	Karns City to Butler	17			
Parker & Karns City	3'	Parker Jct. to Karns City	10.5	1874		
Pitts. New Castle & Lake Erie	3'	Etna to Zelienope	30	1879		
(1)Baltimore & Ohio						
SHADE GAP	3'	Rock Hill to Nancy	11.18	1885		
(1)East Broad Top						

PENNSYLVANIA

NAME	GGE.	TERMINI	MILES	BUILT	S.G.	ABD.
SLATE RUN	3'	Slate Run to Manor Fork	18	1886		1911
SOMERSET COUNTY	3'	Schwerbinz Sta. to Schw. Mill	8.78			1893
SPRING BROOK	4'3"	Moosic to Spring Brook	8.5	1874	1886	
TIONESTA VALLEY RY.	3'	Dunhams to Oglesby	58			1941
		Lomana to Oglesby		1899		
Tionesta Valley	3'	Sheffield to Sheffield Jct.	13	1881		
		Brookston to Annapples	5			
Sheffield & Spring Creek	3'	Sheffield Jct. to Duhrings	11			
Cherry Grove	3'	Sheffield to Garfield	11	1884		
Warren & Farnsworth	3'	Clarendon to Vandergrift	10.05			
		Jct. to Dunhams Mill	4.09	1885		
Warren & Farnsworth Valley	3'	(1882)				
TUSCARORA VALLEY	3'	Port Royal to Blairs Mills	27	1896		1934
WAYNESBURG & WASHINGTON	3'	Washington to Waynesburg	29	1876		
(1)Chartiers (1885)						
(2)Pennsylvania						
WHITE DEER & LOGANTON	3'	Duncan to Loganton	8.8	1907		
White Deer Valley	3'	White Deer to Duncan	15.6	1907		
(1)White D. Lumber Co.(1916)						
YORK & PEACH BOTTOM	3'	York to Peach Bottom	40	1882	1891	
Middle Div. of P. Bottom(1874)						
(1)Md. Central (1889)						

SOUTH CAROLINA

NAME	GGE.	TERMINI	MILES	BUILT	S.G.	ABD.
BRANCHVILLE & BOWMAN	3'11"	Branchville to Bowman	10.5	1893		
CHERAW & CHESTER	3'	Chester to Lancaster	29	1880	1903	
(1)Lancaster & Chester(1896)						
CHESTER & LENOIR (1882)	3'	Chester to Lenoir	109.3	1874	1902	
(A)Kings Mountain						
(1)Chesterville & Yorkville						
(2)Carolina & N.W. (1897)						

SOUTH DAKOTA

NAME	GGE.	TERMINI	MILES	BUILT	S.G.	ABD.
BLACK HILLS & FT. PIERRE	3'	Golden Gate to Piedmont	37.94	1891	1901	
(1)C. B. & Q.						
DEADWOOD CENTRAL	3'	Deadwood to Lead City	3.33	1883		
(1)C. B. & Q. (1892)						
FREMONT ELKHORN & MO. VY.	3'	Deadwood	17.84	1895		
(1) C. & N. W.			2.92			

TENNESSEE

NAME	GGE.	TERMINI	MILES	BUILT	S.G.	ABD.
BROWNSVILLE & OHIO	3'	Brownsville to Friendship	10			1931
(1)Part of Road to Penn. R.R.						
DUCK RIVER VALLEY	3'	Columbia to Fagetteville	48	1882	1890	
(1)N.C. & St. L. (1889)						
E. TENNESSEE & W. N. C.	3'	Jct. Cy. Tenn. to Cranberry N.C.	34	1882		
HOLSTON VALLEY RY.	3'	Bristol to Fields	12.79	1896	1915	
(1)Bristol Traction Co.						
JOHNSON CITY BAKERSVILLE						
& S. RY.	3'	Unicoi to Limestone Cove	10.7	1902		1918
(1)Unicoi Ry. (1909)						
NASHVILLE & TUSCALOOSA	3'	Dickson to Graham	21	1879	1882	
(1)N. C. & St. L. (1880)						
ROCKWOOD & TENN. RIVER	3'		(S.G.1868;N.G.1877)			1911
(1)Roane Iron Company	3'	Rockwood to Tennessee River	5.5			
TENN. & SEQUATCHEE VY.	3'	Spring City to Jewett	12	1882	189-	
(1)Tennessee Central (1888)						
WALDENS RIDGE	3'	Emory Gap to Clinton	45	1882	1888	
(A)Oakdale & Cumberland Mt.						
(1)E. Tenn., Va. & Ga.(1887)						

TEXAS

NAME	GGE.	TERMINI	MILES	BUILT	S.G.	ABD.
AUSTIN & N.W.	3'	Austin to Granite Mtn.	74	1882	1892	
		Granite Mtn. to Marble Falls	16.5	1889		
		Fairland to Llano	29.4	1891-2		
(1)H. & T.C.(SP Co) 1901						
BROWNSVILLE & GULF	3'	Terry Landing to Brownsville	1.01	1889		1900
DURHAM TRANS. CO.	3'	Durham to Spinks	21.	1905	1908	1912
EAST LINE & RED RIVER	3'	Jefferson to Greenville	124.	1876	1883	
(1)M.K. & T. (1881)		Greenville to McKinney	31	1882		
(2)Sherman, Shrev. & S.(1892)						
(3)M.K.T. of Texas (1894)						
ELMINA & E. TRANS. CO.	3'	Elmina to Seaman	10	1904		1910
GALVESTON, BRAZOS & COLO.	3'	Galveston to Westward	15	1876	190-	
(1)Texas-Mexican (1881)						

TEXAS

NAME	GGE.	TERMINI	MILES	BUILT	S.G.	ABD.
GALVESTON, SABINE & ST. L.	3'	Longview Jct. to Martin's Crk.	22	1885	1886	
(1)Tex., Sabine Vy. & NW (1888)						
(2)Texas & Gulf (1904)						
(3)Gulf, Colo. & S. Fe						
GALVESTON & WESTERN	3'	Galveston to Lafitte	13.25	1889		
(1)G.C. & S.F. (1922)(4 Mi. Remaining)						
HOUSTON E. & W. TEXAS	3'	Houston to Goodrich	63	1879	1894	
(See also SHREVEPORT & HOUSTON in La.)		Goodrich to Nacogdoches	75	1880-2	''	
		Nacogdoches to Logansport, La.	54	1883-5	''	
(1)Southern Pacific (1899)						
JEFFERSON & N.W.	3'	Jefferson to Cave Springs	22.5	1902	1909	
KAN. & GULF SHORT LINE	3'	Tyler to Lufkin	95	1885	1886	
(1)St.L., Ark. & Tex.(1887)						
(2)St. Louis, S.W. (1890)						
KILDARE & LINDEN	3'	Kildare to Linden	13.3	1889		1901
LAKE CREEK	3'	Montg. to Hard Thicket	8	1885		1895
POLLOK & ANGELINA VALLEY TRANS. CO.	3'	Pollok to Louis	10			
RIO GRANDE	3'6"	Brownsville to Port Isabel	26.28	1871		1941
(1)Pt. Isabel & Rio Gr. Vy. (1928)						
RIO GR. & PECOS VALLEY	3-rl	Minera to Laredo	30	1882		
(1)Rio Gr. & Eagle Ps.(1889)		(Narrow-gge rail removed 1895)				
TEX. & ST. LOUIS OF TEX.	3'	Texarkana to Mt. Pleasant	128	1880	1887	
(Affiliated with Tex. & St. L		Tyler to Athens	27	1880	''	
in Ark. & Mo. - See "Ark".		Athens to Waco	94	1881	''	
		Waco to Gatesville	46	1882	''	
(A)Tyler Tap (1880)						
(1)St. L., Ark, & Tex. of Tex. (1886)						
(2)St. Louis S.W. (1891)						
TEXAS-MEXICAN	3'	Corpus Christi to San Diego	52	1879	1902	
		San Diego to Laredo	110	1881	''	
(A)Cor. Christi, S.D. & Rio G. Narrow Gauge.						
(1)Operated as Mexi. Nat'l. (1881-88).						
TEX. W. NARROW GAUGE	3'	Houston to Patterson	42	1877		1899
(1)Texas W. Ry. (1880)		Patterson to Sealy	15	1881		''
(2)M.K.T. of Texas (1902)					1902	
WARREN & CORSICANA PAC.	3'	Warren to Campwood & Log Camp	19	1900		1916
(1)Tyler Co. Lbr. Co. (1909)						

UTAH

NAME	GGE.	TERMINI	MILES	BUILT	S.G.	ABD.
AMERICAN FORK	3'	Lehi to Sultana	21	1872		1878
BINGHAM CAN. & CP. FLOYD	3'	Sandy Sta to Bingham City	20	1873		
(A)Wasatch & Jordan Valley						
(1)D. &. R. G. (1882)						
DENV. & RIO GR. W. RY.	3'	Colo. St. Line to Ogden	310.10	1883	1889	
(1)Rio Gr. W. (1889)						
LITTLE COTNWD. TRANS. CO.	3'	Alta to End of Track	20	1923		
SAN PETE VALLEY	3'	Nephi to Wales	30	1882	1896	
		Wales to Big Canyon	3			
SUMMIT COUNTY	3'	Echo to Park City	35.02	1873	188-	
		Watsons to Coal Mines	2.95			
(1)Echo & Park City (1881)						
(2)Union Pacific (1899)						
UTAH & NEVADA	3	S.L. City to Terminus	37	(1881)		
(A)Utah W. Ry. (1875)						
(1)Ore. Short Line & Utah Northern (1889)						
UTAH NORTHERN	3'	Ogden to Franklin	70	1876		
(1)Utah & Northern	3'	Franklin to Sil. Bow Jct., Mont.	338.7	1881		
		Silver Bow Jct. to Butte City	9.42			
		Anaconda Branch	3.60			
		Pocatello to Sil. Box Jct. & Branches			1884	
(2)Ore. Short Line & Utah Northern (1889)						
(3)Ore. Short Line (1897)						
UTAH & PLEASANT VALLEY	3'	Provo to Pleasant Valley	60	1879	Prior to '91	
(1)D.&R.G.W. (1882)					Prior to '91	
WASATCH & JORDAN VALLEY	3'	Brigham City to Alta	33	1876		
(1)R.G.W. (1889)						

VERMONT

NAME	GGE.	TERMINI	MILES	BUILT	S.G.	ABD.
HOOSAC TUNL. & WILM. (1892)	3'	Hoosac Tunl, Mass. to Wilmington, Vt.	24.25	1886		
(A)Deerfield Valley						
WHITE HALL & BRATTLEBORO						
(A)West River		Brattleboro to So. Londonderry	36	1880		1903
(1)New London No.						
(2)Central Vermont						

VIRGINIA

NAME	GGE.	TERMINI	MILES	BUILT	S.G.	ABD.
ATLANTIC & DANVILLE	3'	Claremont to Bellfield	54.5	1885	192-	
		Savidge Branch	6			
(1)Southern (1899)						
DANVILLE & NEW RIVER	3'	Danville to Stuart	75.09	1884	1902	
(1)Danville & W. (1890)						
(2)Southern						
DISMAL SWAMP	3'6"	Camden Mills to Perquimans Co. N.C.	35	1887		1941
FARMVILLE & POWHATAN (1889)	3'	Bermuda to Farmville	39	1890		
		Coalboro to Winterpock	3.14			
		Phaup to Moseley	1.14			
(A)Bright Hope Ry.	3'	Eppes Falls to Bermuda	32.75	S.G. 1858 N.G. 1882		
(1)Tidewater & W. (1905)						
FRANKLIN & PITTSYLVANIA	3'	Pittsylvania to Rocky Mount	29.8	1880	1889	
(A)Pittsylvania						
(1)Virginia Midland (1880)						
(2)Southern (1898)						
LAUREL RY.	3'	Helena to Extraet	1.67	1905		1924
		Lauradale to Mt. City, Tenn.	13.53			
		Laurel Bloomery to Bethel, Tenn.	1			
LONGDALE IRON & COAL CO.	3'6"	Longdale Furn. to Con. C & O Ry	3	1886		1920
MANNS CREEK	3'	Sewell to Clifftop	9			
(1)Babcock Coal & Coke Co. (1913)						
MILTON & SUTHERLAND	3'	Milton, N.C. to Sutherland, Va.	7	1878		1897
NORFOLK & VA. BEACH	3'	Norfolk to Virginia Beach	18	1883	1897	
(1)Nor. Albemarle & Atlan.						
(2)Nor. Va. Bea. & S. (1896)						
(3)Norfolk & Southern (1899)						
NORFOLK & OCEAN VIEW R.R. & HOTEL CO.	3'6½"	Norfolk to Ocean View	8.12	1879		
(1)Va. Ry & Power Co. (1917)						
POTOMAC FREDERICKSBURG & PIEDMONT	3'	Fredericksburg to Orange Co. Court House	38	1874		
(1)Orange & Fredericksburg						
ROCKBRIDGE ALUM SPGS. & VICTORIA & WESTERN	3'	Goshen to Rbdg. Alum Spgs.	12	1892		1905
(1)Rockbridge Alum & Gos.						
SUFFOLK & CAROLINA	3'6"	Suffolk Va. to Montrose, N.C.	39	1874	1907	
(1)Va. & Caro. Coast (1906)						
(2)Norfolk So. (1906)						
SUFFOLK LUMBER CO.	3'6"	Suffolk to Terminus	25	1874		1894
SURRY, SUSSEX & SOUTHAMP.	3'	Scotland to Dory	45	1884		
WHALEYVILLE LMBR. & R.R. CO.	3'	Whaleyville to Suffolk	18			1912

WASHINGTON

NAME	GGE.	TERMINI	MILES	BUILT	S.G.	ABD.
CASCADES	3'	Cascades to Upper Cascades	6	1862		1915
B. 5'Gge. 1862, 4'8½"1880 N.G. 1882						
ILWACO RY & NAV.	3'	Ilwaco to Nahcotta	16	1888		1930
		Holmads to Megler	13.39	1906		
(Ilwaco R.R.)						
(1)O.R. & N. (1900)						
(2)U.P.						
MILL CREEK FLUME & LMBR.	3'	Walla Walla to Dixie & Dudley	16	1881	1897	
(1)O.R. & N. (1896)						
SEATTLE & WALLA WALLA	3'	Seattle to Newcastle	23	1872	1897	
		Renton to Franklin				
(1)Col. & P. Sound (1882)						
THURSTON COUNTY	3'	Tenino to Olympia	17	1878	1891	
(1)Olympia						
(2)Port Townsend So.						
(3)N.P.						
WALLA WALLA & COL. R.	3'	Wallula to Walla Walla	30	1872	1882	
(1)O.R.&N. (1882)		Blue Mountain Branch	10	1879		

WEST VIRGINIA

NAME	GGE.	TERMINI	MILES	BUILT	S.G.	ABD.
BIG SANDY & CUMBERLAND	3'6"	Devon to Grundy Va.	34.11	1914		1932
CAIRO & KANAWHA VALLEY	3'	Cairo to Macfarlan	17	1894		1929
CLARKSBURG WESTON & GLENVILLE	3'	Clarksburg to Weston	26	1879	1890	
(1)W. Va. & Pitts. (1890)						
(2)Baltimore & Ohio (1899)						
CLENDENNIN & SPENCER	3'	Shelley Jct. to Odell	28			1905
GRAFTON & GREENBRIER	3'	Grafton to Phillipi	24	1884	1892	
(1)Grafton & Belington(1892)		Phillipi to Belington	18			
(2)B. & O. (1892)						
KINGWOOD & TUNNELTON RY.	3'	Tunnelton to Kingwood	11	1887	1896	
(1)Tunnelton Kingwood & Fairchance (1888)						
(2)W. Va. Northern (1895)						
PENNSBORO & HARRISVILLE	3'	Pennsboro to Harrisville	9	1875		1924
(1)Pennsboro & Harrisville (Ritchie) Co. Ry. (1880)						
(2)Lorama (1905)						
PICKENS & ADDISON RY.	3'	Pickens - 20 miles	20			1913
(A)Pickens & Webster Spg. Ry.						
PORTERS CREEK & GAULEY	3'	Porter to Middlecreek	30			
RALEIGH & SO. WEST.	3'	Raleigh to end of line (Glade Creek & Raleigh)	18.73			
TWIN MTN. & POTOMAC	3'	Keyser to Twin Mtn.	26.7	1913		1920
VALLEY RIVER	3'	Mill Creek to Elkwater	11			
WESTON & BUCKHANNON	3'	Weston to Buckhannon	15.25	1884	1890	
(1)W. Va. & Pitts. (1890)						
(2)Baltimore & Ohio (1899)						
WEST VA. MIDLAND						1931
(A)Holly River & Addison						

WISCONSIN

NAME	GGE.	TERMINI	MILES	BUILT	S.G.	ABD.
CHICAGO & TOMAH	3'	Woodman to Lancaster	30.5	1878		
		Montfort to Madison	60.84	1881		
		Conley Branch	8	1880		
		Dankliff	13.5	1879		
(1)C. & N.W. (1883)						1926
FOND DU LAC, AMBOY & PEORIA	3'	Fond du Lac to Iron Ridge	28	1877	1883	
(1)C.M. & St.P						
GALENA & SO. WIS.	3'	Galena, Ill. to Platteville	30	1875		
		McCormick's to Phillips	10	1879		
(1)C. & N.W. (1880)						
PINE RIVER VALLEY & STEVENS PT.	3'	Richland Centre to Lone Rock	16	1876	1880	
(1)C.M. & St.P. (1880)						
ROBBINS	3'	Rhinelander to Sugar Camp	12	1904		
(1)Thunder Lake Lumber Co.		Pine Lake to Head of Pine River		1921		1935

(Supplementary List)

ALABAMA

NAME	GGE.	LOCATION	MILES
Smith & Marbury	3'2"	Autauga Co.	7.5
W. D. Carter	3'	Bibb, Shelby & Chilton Co.'s	5
Bivings, Duke & Co.	3'5"	Chilton Co.	8
Miramichi R.R.	4'	Clark Co.	3.25
Harrison, Carter & Co.	4'	Chilton Co.	5.5
Spring Creek Log. Co.	3'	Cherokee Co.	6
Piney Woods Central	3'6"	Chilton Co.	4.5
Warren & Adams	3'	Shelby Co.	3
John B. Randall	3'	Shelby Co.	1.75
Welch & Bro.	3'4"	Chilton Co.	8
A. P. Howison	3'3"	Bibb Co.	8
Talladega & Coosa Vy.	3'	Talladega to Broken Arrow	28
Crowder & Smith	3'	St. Clair Co.	3.5
Gregory & Coe Lmbr.	3'4"	Chilton Co.	9
Hendrix & Smith	3'2"	St. Clair Co.	4
W. W. Wadsworth	3'	Autauga Co.	8
J. R. Adams & Son	3'	Shelby Co.	3.5
W. A. Koeppel	3'	Conn. with the A. G. S.	1.5
Kyle & Elliott Log.	3'	Etowah Co.	8
Marbury & Jones	3'2"	Autanga Co.	11
The Chilton Lmbr. Co.	4'	Chilton Co.	6.5

ARKANSAS

NAME	GGE.	LOCATION	MILES
Brinkley & Helena & Indian Bay	3'	Monroe, Phil. & Lee Co.'s	24
Williams Mills & L. Black River	3'6"	Clay Co.	10
Donaldson Lmbr. Co.	3'	Hot Springs Co.	6
Dry Run Lmbr. Co.	3'	Dallas Co.	1.75
Gifford Lumber Mls. Logging	2'7"	Hot Springs Co.	8
Wyandotte Log. Ry.	2'7"	Hot Springs & Grant Co.'s	8
Vinegar Central	3'	Clark Co.	9
Nathaniel Weston Lumber Co.	3'	Arkansas Co.	1.5
Wrightsville N. G.	3'	Pulaski Co.	11
Lutherville & Col. Mt.	3'	Johnson Co.	3
Malvern Lumber Co.	3'	Hot Springs Co.	7
Solon Ferguson	3'6"	Clay Co.	1.5
Wms'. Mls. & St. Line	3'4"	Clay Co.	6
Pond Cy., Centerville & Northern	3'	Jackson Co.	4.5
Pine City R.R.	3'	Monroe Co.	5
N. Ark. Tram Ry.	4'6"	Sharp & Randolph Co.'s	7.5
Oak Land & Lmbr Co.	3'	White Co.	7
Allen Bros.	3'	Miller Co.	
Wm. Farrell & Co.	3'	Pulaski Co.	6
Field Lmbr Co.	3'	Dalas Co.	4.5
George Griffith	3'	White Co.	7
Paragould & Buffalo Island Ry.	3'	Greene Co.	10

CALIFORNIA

NAME	GGE.	LOCATION	MILES
Towle Bros. & Co.	3'	Placer Co.	22
Andrew Markham	3'	Sonoma Co.	1.5
Sierra Lumber Co.	3'3½"	Tehama & Butte Co.'s	26
Humboldt Lumber Ml. Co. Logging	3'9"	Humboldt Co.	1
Truckee Lumber Co.	3'4"	Placer Co.	2.5
Pac. Lmbr. & Wood Co.	3'	Nevada Co.	9
G. W. Chubback	3'	El Dorado Co.	4

FLORIDA

NAME	GGE.	LOCATION	MILES
Pensac. & Andalusia Branch of the W. Ry. of Florida	3'	Santa Rosa Co.	14
	3'	Clay Co.	13
Hunter's Logging	3'	Clay Co.	13
Geo. W. Robinson Co.	3'	Baldwin Co.	10
E. Fla. Land & Produce Co. Limited	3'	St. John Co.	11.75
Middleburgh High & Lake Butler	3'	Middleburgh to Lake Butler	14

GEORGIA

NAME	GGE.	LOCATION	MILES
Brooks Bros.	3'	Polk Co.	2

KENTUCKY

NAME	GGE.	LOCATION	MILES
John A. Geary	3'	Pulaski Co.	1.5
Bull's Eye Spring Narrow Gauge Ry.	3'6½"	Carter Co.	5
Albion Lumber Co.	3'	Muhlenberg Co.	3

LOUISIANA

NAME	GGE.	LOCATION	MILES
Woodstock Mill	3'	Baton Rouge Parish	4
Octave R. Arbour	3'	9 miles S. of Baton Rouge	2.5
Edgerly Tram Road	3'	Calcasieu P.	4.5
Calcasieu & Vernon	3'4"	Calcasieu P.	21
Dee's Tram No. 1	4'6"	Calcasieu P.	1.5
Robeline & Sabine Pass	3'	Natchitoches P.	8
Amos Kent & Son	3'	Tangipahoa P.	5.5
Gulf, Sabine & Red R.	3'	Calcasieu P.	22
Baton Rouge Pontchatoula & Mobile	3'	Burtville P.	6

MAINE

NAME	GGE.	LOCATION	MILES
Rockport R.R.	3'	Rockport to Simonton's Corner	3

MARYLAND

NAME	GGE.	LOCATION	MILES
Green Ridge of Md.	3'	Okonoko W. Va. to Finksburg Maryland	20

MASSACHUSETTS

NAME	GGE.	LOCATION	MILES
The Armistead Lmbr.	3'	Rankin & Scott Co.	7
B.E. Brister & Co.	3'	Lincoln Co.	5.5
Wesson & Money	3'	Lincoln Co.	6
Morton & Helm	3'	Lincoln Co.	12
W.C. Chamberlin	3'6"	Lincoln Co.	6
H. Lienhurd	3'	Harrison Co.	3
J.J. White	3'	Pike Co.	12
Enoch Bros. R.R.	2'6"	Pike Co.	4.5
C.R. Gage	2	Lincoln Co.	5
Great E. Railroad	3'	Jones Co.	1.5
Whitney & Johnson	3'	Pike Co.	7
Delta Cypress Co.	4'	Bolivar Co.	1
J.P. & W.C. Weatherbee	3'	Wayne Co.	9.5
Keystone Lmbr. & Improvement Co.	3'	Lincoln Co.	17

MICHIGAN

NAME	GGE.	LOCATION	MILES
Alleyton & Big Lake	3'	Newaygo Co.	4.5
Fletcher Pack & Co.	3'	Alcona Co.	9
Arcadia & Betsey R. Tram Co.	3'6½"	Manistee Co.	11
J.E. Potts Salt & Lumber Co.	3'	Osceola Co.	44
Foster, Blackman & Co.	4'	Lake Co.	7
Mecosta R.R.	3'	Mecosta Co.	9
Rumsey Lumber Co.	3'1"	Newaygo Co.	3
Charron & Bourgette	3'	Lake & Mason Cos.	4.5
Cadillac & N. E.	3'	Cadillac to Lake City	15
Cobbs & Mitchell	3'	Wexford and Missaukee Co.'s	5
J. Cummer & Son	3'	Wexford Co.	9.5
Mitchell Bros	3'	Missaukee Co.	10.5
Dunham Peters & Co.	3'	Lake Co.	5
Chippewa L. Log.	4'	Mecosta Co.	8
Cook & Wilson	3'	Chippewa Co.	5.5
Hall & Manning Rd.	3'6"	Lake Co.	3
Edmund Hall	3'	Clare Co.	3
P. Jeannott & Co.	3'	Newaygo Co.	9
Tittabawassee & Hope	3'	Midland Co.	32
J. H. Gibbs	3'	Montcalm Co.	2.5
M. J. Bond	3'	Montcalm Co.	6

MICHIGAN

NAME	GGE.	LOCATION	MILES
C. C. Comstock	3'	Kent, Newaygo Co.'s	5
Copley & Manistee Rd.	3'	Lake Co.	6
A. B. Long & Sons	3'10	Mecosta Co.	8
Daniel McCoy	3'	Lake Co.	4
Portage Lake & Manistee River	3'1"	Crawford Co.	2.5
Ingalls, White Rapids & Northern	3"	Menominee Co.	18
Allegan & Lake Shore	3'	Allegan to Camp	6.5
White Friant & Letellier	3'	Osceola Co.	5
Danaher & Melendy Co.	3'	Newaygo & Lake Co.'s	17
Wilson, Luther & Wilson Logging	3'	Ellsworth Township, Lake Co.	9
Thomas Log & Lmbr.	3'	Montcalm Co.	7
H. M. Harroun	3'	Newaygo Co.	4.5
Crawford & Man. R.	3'	Man. R. to Forest Term.	10
Grass Lake & Man. R.	3'	Man. River to Forest Term.	13.5
Manistee Tram Ry.	3'	Man. & Mason Co.'s	15
Ruddock Nuttal & Co.	3'	Manistee Co.	4.75
Louis Sands	3'2"	Manistee Co.	6
McIntyre & Co.	3'	Iron Co.	3
Wm. Holmes & Son	3'	Iron Co.	4
Midland Tram Ry.	3'	Midland Co.	
Portage Lake	3'½	Roscommon Co.	26
T. D. Stimson	3'	Muskegon Co.	7
West Branch	3'	Missaukee Co.	13
N. Michigan Lmbr. Co.	3'	Newaygo Co.	12
Pelton's Log. Road	3'6"	Lake Co.	4
A. D. Ayers	3'	Newaygo Co.	4.5
Mills & Leighton	3'	Van Buren Co.	2.75
Paris & Pere Marquette	3'	Mecosta Co.	15
Gebhart & Estabrook	3'	Clare Co.	
South Boardman	3'	Kalkaska Co.	8
Cutler & Savidge Lumber Co.	4'	Osceola Co.	6
F. N. Wright & Co.	3'	Montcalm Co.	2
Champion & Hayward	3'	Newaygo Co.	6
Robert Neil	3'	Newaygo Co.	1.5
Staples & Covell	3'	Oceana & Muskegon Co.'s	10
Wingleton & Wolf L.	3'	Lake County	10
Wood Lake Log.	3'	Montcalm Co.	4
Wm. Steel	3'	Montcalm Co.	14.5
Alpena & Hubbard L.	3'	Alpena to Hubbard Lake	18
Lake Mich. & N.	3'	Mackinac Co.	15
Naubinway Logging	3'	Mackinac Co.	12
N. Branch & Sauble	3'	Ludington, Mich	10
Portage Lake & Muskegon River	3'	Grayling, Mich.	38
State Lumber Co.	3'	Kalkaska Co.	16

MISSOURI

NAME	GGE.	LOCATION	MILES
Mo. S. R.R.	3'	Wayne, Reynolds & Carter Co.'s	10
Wm. Egan	3'	Butler Co.	2
H. N. Holladay	4'	Wayne Co.	3.5

NEW YORK

NAME	GGE.	LOCATION	MILES
Chas. Babcock	3'6"	Oswego Co.	2

NORTH CAROLINA

NAME	GGE.	LOCATION	MILES
Bayside & Yaterville	3'6"	Beaufort Co.	6
Camp Mfg. Co.	4'	Hertford Co.	5
E. A. Buell	3'	Hertford Co.	
H. L. Tiiley & Bro.	3'6"	Halifax Co.	2
Chowan & So.	3'6"	Hertford & Bertie Co.'s	26
Dennis Simmons	3'	Martin Co.	4
Roanoke R.R. & Lbr. Co.	3'6"	Beaufort Co.	12
(A)Bayside & Yeatesvle.			

OHIO

NAME	GGE.	LOCATION	MILES
W.C. & J.W. Haskell	3'6"	Ashtabula Co.	3
M.S. Flowers	3'	Paulding Co.	2
Wilson, Fuller & Young	3'8"	Ashtabula Co.	2
Van Wert & Paulding	3'	Van Wert Co.	10

PENNSYLVANIA

NAME	GGE.	LOCATION	MILES
Blossburg Coal Co.	3'	Tioga Co.	3
Piney Run	3'	Somerset Co.	6
Bush & Belknap	3'	Warren & Crawford Co.'s	8.5
Reno R.R.	4'	Forest Co.	5
W.H. Minor	3'	Bradford Co.	1.5
Moore & Andrews	3'6"	Warren Co.	1.25
J.J. Wajenhorst	2'6"	Wayne & Julian Co.	2
Kane Oil Field R.R.	3'	McKean & Elk Co.	7
G.W. Campbell & Co.	3'	McKean Co.	1
E.F. Kizer	2'	Bradford Co.	4
Fox Creek	3'	Nebr. Pa. to Pine Hollow	6
Diamond Valley	3'	Barre to Globe Run. Reed's to Round Top	12.25
Grandin & Slater	3'	Warren Co.	1
Blue Jay	3'	Forest Co.	1.25
D.K. Ramey	3'6"	Clearfield Co.	3.5
Sykes & Caflisch	3'	Elk Co.	2
Jamison Run	4'6"	Forest Co.	2
Tobyhanna & Lehigh Lumber Co.	3'	Monroe Co.	5
Beaver City	3'6"	Crawford Co.	2
Weigel & Co.	4'	Clarion Co.	2
H.A. Bump Co.	3'6"	Susquehanna	2
Wm. Caflish	3'	Elk Co.	3
John Hunter	3'6"	Triumph City	2
Kinzua Crk. & Kane	3'	Kane Co.	9
John B. Moore	2'	Warren Co.	3

SOUTH CAROLINA

NAME	GGE.	LOCATION	MILES
Smoake Tramway Co.	3'	Orangeburg Co.	6
James M. Lumb	3'3"	Hampton Co.	8
R.R. Hudgins	3'	Clarendon Co.	3
Fletcher Mims	3'	Colleton Co.	13
St. John's R.R.	3'	Berkely Co.	10
(A)Summerton & St. John's	3'	Berkely Co.	14

TENNESSEE

NAME	GGE.	LOCATION	MILES
Genesis & Obed Riv.	3'	Cumberland Co.	3
Knob Creek Tram Rd.	3'	Lauderdale Co.	2.5
G.R. Minnick & Co.	3'	Obion Co.	6
L.V. Boyle & Co.	2'11"	Obion Co.	13
Knoxville & New Riv.	3'	Scott Co.	20
Kerville & Big Spring	3'	Tipton & Shelby	6

TEXAS

NAME	GGE.	LOCATION	MILES
W.T. Carter & Bros.	3'	Polk Co.	7.5
Nona Mills Co.	3'	Hardin Co	6
H.R. Smith's Estate	3'	Upsher Co.	3
A.W. Morris	3'	Polk Co.	8
Mathews & Co.	3'	Liberty Co.	6
I. Conroe	3'	Montgomery Co.	3.5
J.K. Ayres	2'4"	Montgomery Co.	2
Lone Star Mill Tram	3'	Polk Co.	4
H.S. Matthew	3'	Eylan, on T.&P., Bowie Co.	5

NAME	GGE.	LOCATION	MILES
Groveton, Kickapoo & Gulf	3'	Trinity Co.	7.5
Angle Lumber Co.	3'	Polk Co.	4
J.S. & W.M. Rice	3'	Tyler Co.	4.5
Jefferson & Cruse	3'	Liberty Co.	5
East. Shore Line	3'	Liberty Co.	9
Atlanta & Mt. Pleasant & Kildare & Linden	3'	Cass Co.	23
Jefferson Lmbr. Co.	3'	Cass Co.	
Sawyer & Son	3'	Polk Co.	2.25
J.L. Garwood	3'	Montgomery	3
C. Bender & Son	3'	Polk Co.	4
W.G. Bering	3'	Polk Co.	9
Olive & Sternerberg Tmbr.	3'	Hardin Co.	6.5
Linden Spg. Bk. & Queen City	3'	Cass Co.	7.5
Seven Oaks Tmbr. Rd.	3'	Polk Co.	6
O.S. Neidigk	3'	San Jacinto Co.	3
Sulphur Lmbr. Co. N.G.	3'	Sulphur Sta.	7.5
W.J. Fowler	3'	Trinity Co.	2
Thompson & Tucker	3'	Trinity Co.	6
Village Mills Co.	3'	Hardin Co.	5.5
Warren Lmbr. Co.	3'	Tyler Co.	8
N. Tex. Land & Tmbr.	3'	Cass Co.	11.5
E. Tex. Trans. Co.	3'	Queen City	8
Tex. Tram & Lmbr.	3'	Hardin, Jasper & Jefferson Co.'s	24

UTAH

NAME	GGE.	LOCATION	MILES
Geo. C. Kidder	2'6"	Wasatch Co.	2
Crescent Mining	2'6"	Park City	4

VIRGINIA

NAME	GGE.	LOCATION	MILES
Moncour Bros.	3'	King William	10
R.F. & W.P. Hill	3'	Orange Co.	2.5
Frank Hitch	3'3"	Bertie Co. N.G.	5
A.L. Nelins	3'	Southampton	5

WASHINGTON

NAME	GGE.	LOCATION	MILES
Musquito & Coal Ck.	3'	Cowlitz Co.	2
Olympia & Chehalis Valley	3'	Tenino to Olympia	25
J.F. Hart & Co.	2'6"	Pierce Co.	3
Col. Riv. & Gray's Harbor	3'	Cowlitz Co.	4

WEST VIRGINIA

NAME	GGE.	LOCATION	MILES
Crowell S. Fewsmith	3'	Ritchie Co.	4
The Hern Lmbr. Co.	3'	Putnam Co.	4.5
St. Lawrence Boom & Mfg. Co.	3'6"	Pocahontas Co.	6

WISCONSIN

NAME	GGE.	LOCATION	MILES
Crescent Spgs.	3'	Washburn Co.	8
S. Range N.G.	3'	Douglas Co.	2

(Supplementary List II)

ALASKA

NAME	GGE.	TERMINI	MILES	BUILT	S.G.	ABD.
WHITE PASS & YUKON	3'	Skagway to Whitehorse, Y.T.	110	1898		
WHITE GOOSE R.R.	3'			1900		
(1) Nome-Artic RR		Nome - Northward		1904		
(2) Seward Peninsula Ry.				1906		
(3) Pioneer Mining Co.				1911		
(4) Territory of Alaska			40	1921		1958
GOLOVIN BAY R.R.	3'		4-5	1902		
(1) Wild Goose RR		Council - Northward				

HAWAII

NAME	GGE.	TERMINI	MILES	BUILT	S.G.	ABD.
HAWAIIAN RR	3'	Mahukona to Niulii	20	1880		
Hawaii Railway				1897		
Makukona Terminals, Ltd.				1937		
KAUAI						
AHUKINIA TERMINAL &	30"	Anahola Landing to Nawiliwili	12	1920		
RAILWAY CO.						
Lihue Plantation				1932		
(private carrier)						
LIHUE RAILWAY CO.	30"	Makaweli to Koloa	19.22	1906		
McBryde Sugar				1933		1947
(private carrier)						
MAUI						
KAHULAI RAILROAD	3'	Wailuku to Kuiaha	16	1879		1967
LAHAINA, KAANAPALI &	3'	Lahaina - North				
PACIFIC RR			16	1969		
Pioneer Mill	30"			1882		1952
OAHU						
KOOLAU RAILWAY	3'	Kahuku to Kahawa	11	1905		
Kahuku Plantation				1931		1954
OAHU RAILWAY & LAND CO.	3'	Honolulu to Kahuku	71.3	1881		1972
						1950 major abandonment
						1950 1970 U.S. Navy
Oahu Railway & Terminal			12	1961		1972
Warehouse Co.						Last switching abandoned in Honolulu

IOWA

NAME	GGE.	TERMINI	MILES	BUILT	S.G.	ABD.
CHICAGO, BELLEVUE,	3'	Bellevue to Cascade	36	1879		1936
CASCADE & WESTERN						
RAILWAY						
(1) Chicago, Clinton, Dubuquet						
Minnesota Railroad (1880)						
(2) Chicago, Milwaukee & St.						
Paul Railway (1880)						
(3) Bellevue & Cascade						
Railroad (1933)						

MONTANA

NAME	GGE.	TERMINI	MILES	BUILT	S.G.	ABD.
GREAT FALLS & CANADA	3'	Sweetgrass (Canada border)	125	1890	1904	
RAILWAY CO.		Virden, Shelby, Conrad				
		Power, Great Falls				

PENNSYLVANIA

NAME	GGE.	TERMINI	MILES	BUILT	S.G.	ABD.
NEW BERLIN &	3'	New Berlin to Winfield	8	1905		1916
WINFIELD RAILROAD						

WASHINGTON

NAME	GGE.	TERMINI	MILES	BUILT	S.G.	ABD.
COLUMBIA & PUGET SOUND	3'	Seattle			1898	
(Originally Olympia						
& Tenino?)						
WALLA WALLA &						
COLUMBIA RIVER RR	3'			1872		
OREGON RAILWAY &	3'	Wallula to Touchet to				
NAVIGATE CO.		Whitman Umalilla to Coyote	43	1880	1881	

CANADA

NAME	GGE.	TERMINI	MILES	BUILT	S.G.	ABD.
ALBERTA						
NORTHWESTERN COAL &		Dynmore Jct. to Ghent to Lethbridge	109	1884	1893	
NAVIGATION CO. LTD.						
ALBERT RAILWAY & COAL CO.		Ghent to Sterling to Coutts	64.6	1890	1903	
ST. MARY'S RIVER RAILWAY CO.		Sterling, Raley to Kimball	45	1900	1903	
		Raley to Carpstow				
BRITISH COLUMBIA						
LENORA MOUNT SICKEN	3'	Vancouver Island	11.5	1901	1907	1912
COPPER CO.		Crofton to Lenora				
(1) Westholme Lumber Co.		a section after		1912	19??	
TRAIL CREEK TRAMWAY	3'	Trail to LeRol	13	1896		
(1) Canadian Pacific				1898	1900	
LAKE LOUISE TRAMWAY	42"	Lake Louise Station (CPR) to	3.6	1912		1931
		Chateau				
KASLO & SLOCAN RAILWAY CO.	3'	Kaslo to Sandon	29	1892	1912	
(1) Canadian Pacific						
NEW BRUNSWICK						
NEW BRUNSWICK RAILWAY	42"	Gibson to Edmundston	190	1870	1881	
NEWFOUNDLAND						
NEWFOUNDLAND RWY.	3' 6"		700+	1881		
(1) Canadian Nat. Rwys.				1949		
MILLERTOWN RAILWAY	3' 6"	Millertown Jct. to Harpoon	38½	1901		1957
(1) Buchans Rwy		to Buchans				
(2) AND Co.			10	1957		
BOTWOOD RWY.	3' 6"					
(1) Grand Falls Center Rwy Co.		Grand Falls to Botwood		1957		
U.S. AIR FORCE	3' 6"	White's Head to Harmon Field	10	1941		1963
NOVA SCOTIA						
LINGAN COLLIERY TRAMWAY	3' 6"	Sidney	1	1861		1866
GLASGOW & CAPE BRETON	3'	Sidney to Schooner Pond	35	1871		
COAL & RWY. CO.		to Louisburg				
PRINCE EDWARD ISLE						
PRINCE EDWARD ISLAND RWY.	3' 6"		196	1870	1930	
ONTARIO						
TORONTO & NIPISSING RWY.	42"	Toronto to Stouffville to Jackson	110	1871		
		Stouffville to Coboconk				
(1) 1881 Midland Railway					1883	
of Canada						
TORONTO, GREG &	42"	Toronto, to Fraxa to Owen Sound	191	1873	1881	
BRUCE RWY. CO.		Fraxa to Teeswater				
HUNTSVILLE, LAKE OF BAYS &	3' 8½"	Huntsville, Ont.	11/8	1902		1963
LAKE SIMCOE RWY. & NAV. CO.						
1951 narrowed	3' 6"					
QUEBEC						
LAKE CHAMPLAIN &	3' 6"	Stambridge to St. Guillaume	56	1879		
ST. LAWRENCE JCT. RWY. CO.						
(1) South Eastern Sys.					1881	
LAKE TEMISCAMINGUE COLONIZATION						
RWY. CO.	3'	Kipawa to Kipawa Landing &	15.2	1886		
		three short tramways				
(1) Canadian Pacific				1891		1893
MONTFORT COLONIZATION RWY.	3'	Montfort to Sixteen Island Lake	21	1893	1898	
YUKON						
WHITE PASS & YUKON	3'	Slagway to Whitehorse	110	1898		
KONDIKE MINES RWY	3'	Dawson City to Sulphur Springs	31.81	1905		1913

BALDWIN
LOCOMOTIVE WORKS.

Burnham, Parry, Williams & Co.,

PHILADELPHIA,

MANUFACTURERS OF

LOCOMOTIVE ENGINES

Adapted to every variety of service, and to the Economical use of Wood, Coke, Bituminous or Anthracite Coal as fuel.

MINE LOCOMOTIVES,

Locomotives for Iron Mills, Furnaces, Contractors' Use, and

Locomotives for Narrow Gauge Railways.

Illustrated Catalogue of Narrow Gauge Locomotives furnished on application.

All work accurately fitted to gauges and thoroughly interchangeable.

Geo. Burnham, Edw. H. Williams, Edw. Longstreth, Chas. T. Parry, Wm. P. Henszey, Jno. H. Converse.

LIGHT LOCOMOTIVES BUILT BY H. K. PORTER & CO., PITTSBURG, PA.

ROGERS
Locomotive & Machine
WORKS,
PATERSON, NEW JERSEY,

Having extensive facilities, are now prepared to furnish promptly, of the best and most approved description, either COAL or WOOD BURNING

Locomotive Engines,
OF ALL GAUGES,

AND OTHER VARIETIES OF

Railroad Machinery.

J. S. ROGERS, President.
R. S. HUGHES, Secretary. } PATERSON, N. J.
WM. S. HUDSON, Supt.

THOS. ROGERS, Treas.,
44 Exchange Place, New York.

PORTER, BELL & CO.,

PITTSBURGH, PENN'A.,

Exclusive Specialty

LIGHT LOCOMOTIVES.

Over 50 Sizes and Styles, from 7x12 to 14x20 Cylinders.

NARROW GAUGE Freight and Passenger Engines for Light or Heavy Equipment.

SPECIAL SERVICE Engines, for Contractors' Use, R. R. Construction and Shifting, Furnaces, Mills, Quarries, Ore, Coal, and Lumber Roads, &c.

MINE LOCOMOTIVES to conform to required dimensions and do the work of 10 to 30 mules, at less than the cost of operating three mules and drivers.

Photograph and Price of Engine to do required work, furnished on application.

NATIONAL
LOCOMOTIVE WORKS.

W. H. BAILEY & CO.,
CONNELLSVILLE, PA.

MANUFACTURERS OF

LOCOMOTIVE ENGINES,

Of the best and most approved description, and adapted to every kind of service, to burn either wood or coal.

Locomotives for Furnaces, Iron Mills, Contractors' Use, and Mine Locomotives.

NARROW GAUGE LOCOMOTIVES

A SPECIALTY,

All parts built to a standard gauge and thoroughly interchangeable.

Material, Workmanship, Finish, and Efficiency fully guaranteed. Photographs and Specifications furnished on application. Correspondence Solicited.

Office and Works at Connellsville, Pa.

BILLMEYER & SMALLS'
YORK CAR WORKS,

ADJOINING NORTHERN CENTRAL AND PENNSYLVANIA RAILROAD DEPOTS,

YORK, PENN'A

UNITED STATES OF AMERICA.

BUILDERS OF

BROAD AND NARROW GAUGE CARS.

York, Pa., February, 1875.

We take pleasure in referring to the FOLLOWING ADDITIONAL NARROW-GAUGE RAILROADS, which have been supplied with Cars from our Works:

PARKER AND KARNS CITY, Pennsylvania.
BINGHAM CANYON AND CAMP FLOYD, Utah.
MINERAL RANGE, Michigan.
EUREKA AND PALISADE, Nevada.
LONGDALE IRON COMPANY, Virginia.
OHIO AND TOLEDO, Ohio.
IOWA EASTERN, Iowa.

PEACHBOTTOM R. W., Pennsylvania.
PITTSBURG AND CASTLE SHANNON, Pennsylvania.
MEMPHIS AND RALEIGH, Tennessee.
NEW CASTLE R. R. AND MINING COMPANY, Pennsylvania.
MILLWOOD COAL AND COKE COMPANY, Pennsylvania.
BELL'S GAP R. R., Pennsylvania.
TROCHA DEL ESTE, Cuba.

Following we give a general description of our Narrow-gauge Cars, each style of Car being designated by a letter in the alphabet, so that in describing them they may more easily be recognized.

CAR X, is an Eight-wheeled Double Drop Bottom Patent Coal Car. Weight about nine thousand (9000) pounds. Capacity, eighteen thousand (18,000) pounds. Will relieve itself of its load without shoveling and can be adapted to carry coke, lime and ores.

CAR Q, is an Eight-wheeled Gondola Car with seats made of plank fastened to top of sides, with a covering and arm rests on the side of the standards, which can easily be removed when desired to use as a freight car and replaced at any time. This car will seat 50 to 60 passengers; is used for excursions. Swinging bolster trucks can be used, as under car Y, at a small additional cost.

CAR J, is a Third Class or Emigrant Passenger Car, seating twenty-six (26) passengers alongside of car facing each other. Length, in body twenty-two (22) feet, width, seven and a half (7½) feet. This car can be made longer to carry more passengers and either narrower or wider with only a small additional expense.

CAR M, Combination Second Class Passenger Car, one-third (⅓) for baggage and two-thirds (⅔) for passengers, seating twenty-four (24) passengers alongside of car with slat or cushioned seats, as preferred, saloon, lamps, stove, water cooler, and all other necessary conveniences. Length in body thirty (30) feet; length over all thirty-six (36) feet; width seven (7) feet; can be built seven and a half to eight (8) feet wide, with seats in regular way reversible or stationary as preferred. These cars have 24 inch wheels and 3⅜ inch axles.

Car M M, is a Second Class Passenger Car 6½ feet wide, seating 36 passengers side-ways facing each other, is 30 feet long or 36 feet over all. By adding 5 feet more to its length it will seat 44 passengers. It can be made 7 feet wide and 35 feet long and seat 36 passengers, with reversible seats 3 abreast, half the number of seats for 2 passengers and the other half for 1 passenger,—or by making car 8 feet wide will seat 4 abreast, i. e., 2 seats of two passengers each, and seat 47 passengers.

The above cut represents a First-Class Passenger Car seven feet wide. Length of body 35 feet, length over all 41 feet, will comfortably seat 36 passengers. The seats are double on one side and single on the other, this arrangement being reversed in the centre of the car, so that each side carries half double and half single seats, which secures a proper balance of weight when the car is full. By adding one foot to width of car we can make all the seats double on each side, seating 4 abreast, and will seat 47 passengers. This car is mounted on our "Patented Truck" with 24 inch wheels and 3⅜ inch axles.

CAR Z, a Four-wheeled Side Dump Car. Weight about forty-five hundred (4500) pounds. Capacity, nine thousand (9000) pounds of lime, limestone, iron and silver ore. These cars are extensively used to carry silver and other ores in the Rocky Mountains, and for lime, limestone and iron ore in Penn'a., can be easily dumped at any point on either side of track without detaching car from train, are made perfectly secure by our improved supports and stays from danger of tilting while in motion.

CAR T, is a Four-wheeled Dump Coal Car, intended to run in large trains and on long lines. Length, twelve (12) feet. Height from top of rail five (5) feet four (4) inches. Weight, about forty-five hundred (4500) pounds. Capacity, nine thousand (9000) pounds.

CAR V, is a Four-wheeled Mining Dump Car.   Weight, about twenty-two hundred (2200) pounds.   Capacity, (heaped up) forty-five hundred (4500) pounds.   This car can be built to carry fifty-five hundred (5500) pounds by adding to height of car.   It has eighteen (18) inch "chilled" wheels, suitable for running into mines and on short lines behind a small locomotive or drawn by mules; they are used extensively on the coal roads in Pennsylvania and Ohio.

CAR Y, is a First-Class Baggage and Express Car, with swing bolster.   It can be built seven and a half (7½) to eight (8) feet wide, increasing its carrying capacity.   The car as shown in above cut is seven (7) feet wide.